Acc no: 4352

Class :

INTERPERSONAL
CONFLICTS
AT WORK

Robert J. Edelmann

Personal and Professional Development

INTERPERSONAL CONFLICTS AT WORK

Robert J. Edelmann

Lecturer in Clinical Psychology
University of Surrey

 Published by The British Psychological Society

First published in 1993 by BPS Books (The British Psychological Society),
St Andrews House, 48 Princess Road East, Leicester LE1 7DR.

A catalogue record for this book is available from the British Library.

ISBN 1 85433 087 X paperback
ISBN 1 85433 086 1 hardback

Typeset by Litho Link Limited, Welshpool, Powys, Wales
Printed in Great Britain by BPCC Wheatons Ltd, Exeter

Personal and Professional Development

Series Editors:

Glynis M. Breakwell is Professor of Psychology and Head of the Psychology Department at the University of Surrey.

David Fontana is Reader in Educational Psychology at University of Wales College of Cardiff.

Glenys Parry is Director of Psychology Services for Sheffield Health Authority.

The books in this series are designed to help readers use psychological insights, theories and methods to address issues which arise regularly in their own personal and professional lives and which affect how they manage their jobs and careers. Psychologists have a great deal to say about how to improve work styles. The emphasis in this series is upon presenting psychology in a way which is easily understood and usable. We are committed to enabling our readers to use psychology, applying it for themselves to themselves.

The books adopt a highly practical approach. Readers are confronted with examples and exercises which require them to analyse their own situation and review carefully what they think, feel and do. Such analyses are necessary precursors in coming to an understanding of where and what changes are needed, or can reasonably be made.

These books do not reflect any single approach in psychology. The editors come respectively from social, educational and clinical branches of the discipline. They work together with the authors to ensure that each book provides a fair and comprehensive review of the psychology relevant to the issues discussed.

Each book deals with a clearly defined target and can stand alone. But combined they form an integrated and broad resource, making wide areas of psychological expertise more freely accessible.

OTHER TITLES IN THE SERIES
Managing Time by David Fontana

Contents

For Mary Bernadette:
Thank you for everything (again).
Also for Genevieve Rebecca Mary: born into the chaos;
May you never have serious interpersonal
conflicts at work.
And for Lynne and Ann,
who unfortunately have

Chapter One

Causes and Consequences of Interpersonal Conflicts

A considerable proportion of our lives is spent at work – seven to eight hours or more for five or more days each week for between 40 to 45 years. Some 100 000 hours during our lives! A great deal of this time will be spent working with others. Some of those we work with and with whom we share interests and activities away from the work environment will also be our friends. In surveys of friendships, however, less than a quarter of those we consider to be friends are also those we work with, and as many as half of us do not have any friends at work. Workmates are those we are brought into contact with because of the nature of our employment and may not be the same as those people we voluntarily choose to spend time with away from work. Nevertheless, work relationships are very important and can be a source of satisfaction and support when they run smoothly. Supportive relationships at work are frequently associated with a far lower incidence of employee anxiety, depression and physical illness. However, relationships at work can be a source of great distress and dissatisfaction when conflicts do occur.

Conflicts at work are certainly not uncommon, minor disagreements or heated discussions being inevitable aspects of most work environments. Indeed, such conflicts can be productive if they generate creative solutions, and are, in fact, compatible with high levels of work satisfaction. However, when differences and disagreements, whether real or imagined, provoke ill feeling, they can result in long-term stress and unhappiness. Rather than being resolved, such interpersonal difficulties can endure and escalate. This is particularly true when one person creates the difficulty, while at the same time failing to acknowledge that a difficulty exists; for example, a boss who unreasonably criticizes our efforts or who makes unmanageable demands, a colleague who exceeds their authority or who excludes us from information, or a client who makes excessive demands on our time. Other interactions may be complicated by sexual innuendos or unwelcome sexual advances, or because of discriminatory remarks or behaviour. Our initial reaction to such behaviour from others may be to blame ourselves, feeling as if we are in some way responsible for its occurrence. Some criticisms or instances of harassment are so unexpected that we fail to cope with them effectively at the time, leaving us feeling inadequate. We may subsequently feel angry, both with the other person for creating the situation, and also with ourselves for not confronting it.

This book will examine some of the sources of conflict in our relationships at work as well as why conflicts arise, the effect they can have on our personal well-being and the ways in which we can attempt to deal with them. It is important to recognize, however, that not all conflicts can be resolved. With minor disagreements, it is perfectly acceptable to agree to disagree. In other instances, any attempt to resolve a conflict clearly necessitates an effort on both sides if it is to succeed. It is important to recognize:

There is a limit to your responsibility. If you try to address the problem but fail because the other person is unwilling to co-operate, you have clearly done what you can under the circumstances. Avoid undermining your own confidence by either blaming yourself for the initial conflict and/or for your failure to resolve it.

If a conflict persists, you may wish to review your work-related options. This may involve investigating formal complaints procedures, seeking a transfer to another department or unit or, as a last resort, changing jobs. Clearly, which options are viable will depend on a variety of factors. This book should help you to find appropriate strategies to resolve interpersonal conflicts at work. The final chapter, in particular, examines the options available when conflicts persist.

This chapter examines the nature of work relationships as well as possible sources of conflict. Group processes, relationships rules, aspects of power and leadership and gender and personality differences all serve to shape our relationships and offer clues to why conflicts occur. The way we perceive and deal with these issues will determine whether such conflicts have a negative or positive outcome.

EFFECTS OF CONFLICTS AT WORK

A broad range of factors can make our lives at work more or less stressful. These can be summarized as follows:

- Factors determined by the nature of the job itself, such as too much or too little work.
- Factors resulting from one's role within the organization, such as level of responsibility.
- Factors intrinsic to the organizational structure, such as a lack of consultation.
- Issues relating to career development, such as thwarted ambition.
- Factors involving the nature of relationships with one's boss, subordinates, colleagues or clients/patients, etc.

Indeed, the first four factors may also be related to poor working relationships. Lack of consultation, uncertainty about the level of one's responsibility, failure to gain promotion (or failure to gain promotion before others whom we perceive to be less deserving) may all result from or exacerbate conflicts with those with whom we work.

NEGATIVE EFFECTS

Work environments are frequently characterized by a range of destructive conflicts with consequent negative effects. These include damage to physical and emotional well-being, loss of confidence and lowered self-esteem. Clearly, the magnitude of such effects will depend upon the nature of the conflict, its personal importance and its duration. It may be possible to ignore a minor conflict in the hope that it will go away; indeed, as long as both parties forgive and forget this may well occur. However, even a seemingly minor conflict may not be perceived as such by both parties, leading to the conflict developing unnecessarily. Major conflicts which are usually evident to both parties, even though their perception of events might differ, are most likely to have negative psychological repercussions.

The negative effects of interpersonal conflicts at work are evident at both a personal and organizational level. In the latter instance, conflict has been shown to affect the performance of the organization or unit as a whole. In the former instance, negative effects of interpersonal conflict are most likely to be stress-related with the person showing psychological, physical and behavioural symptoms.

At the *psychological level*, common reactions include an inability to concentrate and think clearly, with an increase in irritability and an inability to relax.

Minor *physical ailments* such as headaches, difficulty sleeping and upset stomachs are also early warning signs which, if left unheeded, may lead to ulcers and high blood pressure.

Behavioural signs may involve withdrawal from relationships which are proving difficult, in addition to the overuse of alcohol, cigarettes or tranquillizers in an attempt to relieve tension. (For a full description of stress-related reactions, see Fontana, 1989.)

Indeed, there is often a vicious cycle with conflicts leading to stress, which in turn results in an increase in cynicism about clients or colleagues, leading to further conflict. Such reactions may reduce the likelihood that events will be perceived objectively and increase the likelihood that they will be seen as being beyond one's control with the blame being attributed solely to others. Managing interpersonal conflicts thus plays an important role in reducing stress at work.

POSITIVE EFFECTS

Less well documented is the fact that conflicts at work, when systematically dealt with, can have positive rather than destructive effects.

☐ *Strengthening a relationship.* If two people are able to recognize that they have differences, understand why they have occurred and discuss and resolve them, the work relationship will be stronger as a result.

☐ *Greater trust.* If two people can resolve a conflict, they are more likely to trust each other in the future knowing that their differences can be dealt with.

☐ *Increased self-esteem.* The productive outcome from any conflict is likely to result in increased self-esteem for the parties concerned.

☐ *Enhancing creativity and productivity.* It has been suggested that conflict, effectively managed, is a necessary condition for creativity and that discussion between people with differing interests or opinions can lead to increased productivity.

□ *Job satisfaction*. Some writers have speculated that people need a certain amount of stimulation, and use the continuing experience of tension generation and reduction, within limits, in order to function well and to retain job satisfaction. One writer (Deutsch, 1971) has gone even further, arguing that for some people and in certain instances, conflict serves to stimulate interest and curiosity, leading to the full use of the individual's capacities and acting as a welcome means for testing and assessing one's abilities.

Clearly such positive effects are only likely if conflict is limited or controlled. The nature of conflicts and their resolution will also be influenced by our general pattern of relationships at work and our perception and interpretation of conflict-related events.

SATISFACTION IN WORKING RELATIONSHIPS

Working relationships can function as a source of support, satisfaction and/or friendship. A supportive relationship is generally one which is also likely to be satisfying. A work relationship may not necessarily develop into a social friendship and, indeed, does not need to do so in order for it to be a source of satisfaction and support.

Satisfaction with work relationships is closely related to overall job satisfaction which, in turn, is related to overall life satisfaction. Yet, as Argyle and Henderson (1985) note, work relationships are often seen as superficial and as more likely to lead to conflict in comparison to relationships with friends or family. Expectations of work relationships clearly differ from those associated with other relationships. As Argyle and Henderson further note, we are more likely to expect personal growth and financial rewards from our work relationships, while in friendships the other person or the relationship itself are the focus of our concern. For the most part, our work relationships are task-oriented and formal. Satisfaction increases when they are also co-operative and friendly. Competitive relationships at work, however, are not uncommon, especially between those of marginally differing status. Competition can be conducted in a friendly manner and is not, in itself, a necessary precursor of conflict, particularly if it results in both parties furthering their aims. Relationships at work also vary in their intensity; those involving clients or pupils demand more intense input than those involving co-workers. Indeed, more satisfaction may be gained from helping relationships than those involving colleagues.

A number of theoretical models in psychology have attempted to explain the differing levels of satisfaction with relationships in terms of a balance between rewards and costs. According to *equity theory* (Walster *et al.*, 1978), the most satisfying relationships are those where you gain as much as you put in. Applied to the work context, a satisfying relationship with a colleague would be one in which both parties know they can rely on each other to take their fair share of responsibility, share the workload and co-operate in joint tasks. Equity theory would hold that the introduction of an imbalance or inequity would lead to a decrease in satisfaction. However, in many work contexts, a colleague may prefer to take additional responsibility, perhaps with the aim of securing promotion. As long as both parties believe that what they are receiving is fair, a perfect balance in a work relationship is not necessary for it to be regarded as satisfying.

According to the *investment model* (Rusbult, 1983) we will be more satisfied with relationships which provide high rewards and low costs and which exceed our expectations. This theory can be applied to certain superior–subordinate relationships at work. A satisfying relationship with a superior may be one where, as well as being directed in our work, we acquire knowledge and skills from them, while in return we provide co-operative work input. A boss who acts as a mentor by developing our skills, can certainly play an influential role in our subsequent career development.

Work relationships primarily involve the giving and receiving of help and support with shared tasks and other formal activities. A degree of perceived fairness in our dealings with others minimizes conflict. Given that two people's goals are unlikely to be wholly compatible in all aspects of their work at all times, some degree of conflict is inevitable. Indeed, as noted, some might argue that a degree of conflict is desirable and can be constructive if both parties share the common goals of working together and trusting each other. Conflict is destructive if important goals conflict, if trust is minimal and if both parties do not take responsibility for resolving differences.

WHY DO CONFLICTS ARISE?

For many people, a major part of their working day is spent interacting with other people. A survey of British firms conducted during the 1960s (Stewart, 1967) found that as much as 90 per cent of managers' time was spent with others. This figure may well be exceeded by members of professional groups outside of industry, such as the police or those involved in education or health. Indeed, in many such jobs it may be rare to spend time alone.

Our contact with people at work can clearly take many forms. Depending upon the nature of our employment and our status within the organization, we may relate to colleagues, supervisors or supervisees. In addition, we may interact with clients, pupils or the general public. In the course of such interactions, we may receive and give instructions, co-operate and negotiate, or we may teach, interview and inform or help others to deal with their problems. All such relationships are determined by the formal structure of the working environment, while their smooth functioning is determined by an informal rule base. Non-adherence to this rule base is one of the major determinants of conflict in working relationships.

There are, however, a range of factors which can determine whether conflicts will arise or whether our working relationships with others will be harmonious. Issues which need to be considered are group characteristics, relationship rules, inter-personal differences, how we treat others and how we perceive particular situations. These factors can be summarized as follows:

Factors inherent in groups at work:
- the formation of cliques
- group pressure and stereotypes

Factors inherent in the relationship:
- patterns of communication
- breaking relationship rules

Factors inherent in the people concerned:
- a personality 'clash'
- gender and age differences

Factors inherent in our evaluation and treatment of others:
- assumptions about others
- misuse of authority
- power tactics and manipulation

Factors inherent in our evaluation of the situation:
- general expectations and beliefs
- misunderstandings
- unreasonable beliefs and assumptions.

GROUP CHARACTERISTICS

As with social relationships, groups can be either formal, created to accomplish a particular task, or informal, based upon either real or assumed common interests or activities. There is inevitably overlap between such groups. Within both the work environment and the broader social context, there are also more loosely knit groups based upon factors such as age, religion, race, gender or sexual orientation.

All work environments encourage, to varying degrees, the establishment of informal relationships. This may take the form of interactions during coffee or lunch breaks, or during sporting and social activities facilitated by the organization concerned. While working relationships are established by the formal system of work, people engage in informal social activity with a specific subgroup of work colleagues, most usually those with whom they share interests other than work or those whom they like. Such informal contacts may develop into social friendships. This tends to be more common in certain professions, particularly where contacts with clients is important or where work is a central life interest. Working in shifts or other specific working practices may also increase the likelihood of forming social friendships with work colleagues.

The establishment of informal relationships or social friendships with work colleagues can have both positive and negative repercussions on the general pattern of working relationships within organizations. Informal relationships may facilitate co-operation at work. However, they may also lead to the formation of subgroups or cliques with potentially negative results. Conflict may arise when a person feels excluded from an informal network of which they would like to be a part. A subgroup may exclude outsiders from information or decision-making, diminish outsiders' responsibility and gradually isolate them. The existence of groups, both at work and in the broader social context, can thus serve to generate and maintain interpersonal conflicts at work. As Frank, a 30-year-old teacher, explains:

❏ *There is a small group of staff whom we call the 'crossword addicts'. They sit in the same place in the staff room every lunch time completing crosswords together, while discussing work-related matters. The people concerned teach the same year group as me and I need to discuss organizational issues with them, yet this is impossible unless I join their lunch time group. Unfortunately I don't like crosswords and feel rather left out of things, both socially and when decisions are made about work.*

One factor in relation to groups which has received a great deal of research interest is the notion of *group cohesiveness* – the feeling of belongingness or shared understanding of group members. Long-standing groups with established patterns of interacting are likely to be more cohesive. In general, as the cohesiveness of a group increases, so does the overall level of conformity of group members to the norms of that group. Cohesiveness can clearly have positive effects; research suggests that satisfaction is greatest in cohesive groups. However, cohesiveness is not only associated with strong positive feelings towards other group members, it is also associated with negative attitudes towards outsiders.

A number of factors which make groups more or less cohesive have been identified, one of which is *perceived external threat*. In settings where groups compete with one another or where members perceive outsiders as posing a threat to established norms, the solidarity and morale of members within groups tends to increase, while hostility grows between groups. Unfortunately, group membership is often used as an excuse to exclude people of different religions, race or gender from access to information, promotion or even to employment. It is certainly not uncommon for women working in male-dominated environments such as industry or the police force to feel excluded. As Angela, a 25-year-old police officer, comments:

❏ *I feel as if I have a stark choice: either I have to fight to retain my female identity, in which case I am often ignored by male colleagues, or I have to behave like 'one of the boys', engaging in all the 'macho' activity.*

The converse situation may arise in nursing or primary education where men may find themselves in female-dominated environments with similar problems arising from group exclusion.

A further factor related to group membership is the notion of *stereotypes;* the idea that a person possesses a certain set of attributes merely because they belong to a specific subgroup of society. It is not unusual for stereotypical notions to be inherently negative. They are thus often used by groups who perceive themselves as dominant (although in reality this is not necessarily the case) to maintain their assumed position, particularly if they perceive it as being under threat. In this way gender and racial stereotypes may serve as a basis for discrimination and harassment; as do stereotypes relating to older or younger workers, lesbians, gays and disabled workers.

RELATIONSHIP RULES

All our relationships are governed by a set of informal rules, the behaviour most people think is appropriate or inappropriate in a particular context. These rules guide and co-ordinate our behaviour and help to prevent difficulties and conflict. Breaking the rules may result in the failure or disruption of a relationship unless the damage is repaired. Some rules are universal to all relationships; others are particular to specific work relationships. The latter will be referred to in subsequent chapters where appropriate. (A more detailed account of the rules of relationships is provided in Argyle and Henderson, 1985.) The following general rule categories can be applied to all work contexts:

☐ *Rules of support.* Within work relationships, the most common form of support relates to practical concerns although emotional support may also be involved. This is true of relationships between colleagues, even if these do not develop into social friendships, superior–subordinate relationships and, in a somewhat different form, between professionals and their clients or patients. It is therefore assumed that we will offer colleagues practical help on a work-related task, that we will stand in for colleagues in their absence, that we will give advice, encouragement or guidance to subordinates or patients/clients and so on.

☐ *Rules of intimacy.* A number of rules relating to intimacy apply to all work relationships. These include respecting the other person's privacy and refraining from engaging in sexual activity with subordinates or within professional relationships. In the latter case, the profession's own ethical guidelines act as a guard against such practice. It is also assumed that we will refrain from sexual activity with co-workers unless we receive their active encouragement or agreement, and as long as this does not interfere with working practices. Instances of sexual harassment ranging from sexual innuendos to unwanted sexual contact all involve transgressing intimacy rules relating to work relationships.

☐ *Rules relating to third parties.* Relationships between people at work do not exist in isolation from the broader social context. Others not involved in our day-to-day interactions can have a major effect on our immediate relationships. Thus, we should not criticize others in public, nor should we discuss with others what has been told to us in confidence. It is also assumed that we should stand up for colleagues in their absence.

☐ *Task-related rules.* All professional relationships, whether teacher–pupil, therapist–client, nurse–patient or police officer–general public, are largely governed by rules which relate to the completion of specific tasks. For example, doctors are expected to diagnose and treat or advise; teachers are expected to prepare lessons, plan and assign work; counsellors are expected to listen and advise and so on. There are also task-related rules for the recipients of professional advice/tuition, such as the need for a student to submit assignments at specified times or the need for patients/clients to provide information. In general, an understanding of the rules is shared by both parties or is clarified by the professional concerned. Clearly, however, misperceptions, misunderstandings or disagreements about the way the task should be conducted do occur.

Given that all our work relationships are governed by informal rules, adhering to these rules minimizes potential sources of conflict. Conversely, knowing which rule has been broken will go some way towards explaining why the conflict has arisen. Any public criticism of someone we work with, a failure to show respect for that person's privacy or to keep a confidence will cause difficulty in work or professional relationships. As Dawn, a social worker, comments:

One of my immediate colleagues has taken an obvious dislike to me; she gossips about me behind my back and comments to other colleagues about my ability. I would rather she was rude to my face, at least I could tell her what I think.

Similarly, a superior who fails to inform or involve subordinates in decision-making, a co-worker who refuses to co-operate or a client or professional who steps beyond acceptable levels of intimacy, is likely to create conflict in the relationships concerned.

PERSONALITY CLASH

It is often assumed that our behaviour is determined as much by our inherent personality characteristics as it is by circumstances or events in our environment. Indeed, most current research emphasizes an interaction between the personality characteristics we bring to any situation, the concrete aspects of the situation itself and our interrelations with other people. One personality attribute which is important for leadership roles and for many jobs, particularly those in health and education, is flexibility, the ability to be adaptive in order to meet the demands of varying situations. Jobs with more defined rules and more obvious criteria inevitably require less flexibility.

A common assumption is that particular occupations will attract individuals with similar personality attributes, as exemplified by the stereotypes of the warm-hearted therapist or the hard-headed businessman. Indeed, it is reasonable to assume that people with certain personality types might be more inclined to look for particular jobs and, that once in such jobs, they would gain greater satisfaction from them than people with other personality types. Certainly, vocational guidance pays much attention to such factors.

In spite of this, it is obvious that people in the same work environments are very different from each other. There are inevitably those we like and work well with, even though we have little in common with them. At the other end of the spectrum, are those with whom we find it difficult to interact and with whom we are likely to clash over seemingly trivial matters. As Simon, a police officer, comments:

❏ *When Steve and I are on the same shift we just try to get on with the work, keeping everything as formal as possible. It's difficult to say why we don't get on, we just seem to irritate each other.*

Few people are simply considered as difficult to work with by most people; the majority of clashes are between two people who approach the same situation in different ways. For example, someone who is very fixed in their way of working would find it difficult to work with someone who is very flexible; someone who is conscientious would find it difficult to work with someone who is rather more 'laid back' in their approach. We may clash with someone because of differing opinions or beliefs or because of a dislike of personal habits. However, it is possible to work with people we dislike simply by adhering to the appropriate relationship rules and by treating them with respect and courtesy.

GENDER DIFFERENCES

There are many ways in which gender can impinge upon working practice and work relationships. A number of studies suggest that women find their jobs more satisfying but, at the same time, more stressful than men do. It is frequently found that women have more friends at work, but also more people whom they do not get on with. In order to succeed, women often feel that they have to be better at their jobs than their male counterparts and are, in fact, often better qualified than males in equivalent positions. As noted, women in male-dominated organizations may encounter particular difficulties by being excluded from social activities as well as from decision-making ventures.

Clearly, the difficulties women experience at work cannot be separated from the broader social context. Men still predominate in positions of economic privilege and higher status, and this reflects the social power balance in which men are regarded as being dominant and women subdominant or 'muted'. Many have argued that sex role stereotypes serve to maintain this power balance, by setting up norms and expectations which constrain men and women by limiting the behaviours which will be regarded as appropriate. For instance, men are rewarded for assertive and aggressive behaviour while women are rewarded for acquiescent, compliant and passive behaviour. Indeed, our heroes and heroines reflect the contrasting 'masculine' and 'feminine' ideals; typical heroes being rugged sportsmen or intrepid adventurers and typical heroines being supportive wives, caring mothers or innocent maidens.

'Sex role spillover' is the term used to denote the inappropriate reference to sex role stereotypes in the workplace (Gutek and Morasch, 1982). Conflicts at work can arise because of pressure to adopt and play out particular sex role behaviours or because some people find it difficult to relinquish their fixed assumptions about what constitutes 'normal' male or female behaviour. Kanter (1979) has identified four stereotypical roles which are often assigned to women within the workplace and which all serve to diminish their competence and integrity as serious working people. The 'mother earth' role defines women as nurturant and caring and sets up the expectation that they will behave as such at work. Many women may accept this role as an intrinsic part of their job, others may be forced into it by male colleagues. The 'seductress' role, on the other hand, defines women as sex objects who are there to titillate men rather than to work. Some women may choose to play along with this, but it is clearly not in the interests of women who wish to be viewed as professional working women. Women who find themselves in the 'pet' role are either just tolerated or are treated as decoration rather than as equals. Indeed, women are placed in a double-bind, for if they do not accept one of the other three roles, they are identified as 'iron maidens' – tough, dangerous and unfeminine.

One of the most serious problems relating to gender in the workplace is that of sexual harassment. Many have argued that harassment is intimately bound up with issues of power and must be seen as a means whereby males can retain their position of dominance, both within society at large and in the workplace. This will be dealt with further in Chapter 5.

AGE DIFFERENCES

As with gender, age-based stereotypes influence our perception of and reaction towards those with whom we work. Indeed, ageism is such that recruitment policies for many organizations favour the young. This is no doubt fuelled by stereotypical notions of younger people as inventive and flexible, while older people are seen as conservative and inflexible. This is in spite of the fact that available evidence suggests that older workers have lower absenteeism, turnover, illness, and accident rates; higher job satisfaction; and more positive work values (Rhodes, 1983). Real age differences do exist; older workers tend to be more experienced and are often in senior positions, younger workers tend to have more up-to-date training and knowledge. In many such instances, separating authority from knowledge can be a major source of conflict at work. Equal status colleagues of different ages may feel that their greater experience or knowledge give them the natural edge. The younger worker may feel aggrieved if his or her knowledge is not taken into account when given instructions by an older manager; conversely, an older, more experienced person may fail to respond to a possibly more knowledgeable, but inexperienced, younger manager.

In addition, with the ever increasing technological innovations at work, the need for retraining has never been greater. While stereotypical notions that older people are conservative and in-flexible are inherently incorrect, it is nevertheless difficult for many people to learn new skills or to adopt new working practices. Keeping pace with change or admitting to gaps in one's knowledge can also present problems. It can be difficult for older employees to work alongside younger colleagues who already possess such skills or to ask a younger, inexperienced colleague for advice. We may feel that they will perceive us negatively, although they may actually respect our experience and be pleased that we have chosen to ask them for help.

HOW WE PERCEIVE THE SITUATION

MISPERCEPTIONS AND MISUNDERSTANDINGS

Conflicts are seldom clearcut. Each party has their own perceptions and understandings of an event and these may differ markedly from each other. It may, at first, appear as if there is little ambiguity about a situation. If a superior repeatedly criticizes our efforts in public, it would seem to be a clear example of mismanagement. A colleague who refuses to do their work is placing an unfair burden of responsibility on someone else. However, most situations are more ambiguous. Was the criticism intended? Is the colleague's work role clearly defined or are they unaware of their responsibilities?

Two factors are involved in any realistic assessment of events; first, a careful analysis of the situation is required and, second, it is important to try to understand the viewpoint of the other person. It might be worthwhile to confront the other person, both to let them know that you found their behaviour undesirable and to establish their degree of intent. You may find that the behaviour was unintentional and the conflict can be easily resolved. Difficulties in interpretation or perception of an event are perhaps more difficult to resolve. A third party, perhaps a mutual superior or a union representative, could be approached to act as a mediator (see Chapter 6) or, as mentioned, you might be able to agree to differ over a minor conflict. Clearly, however, people will have their own particular way of perceiving events and one should continually strive to respect all views in the work environment.

EXPECTATIONS AND BELIEFS

Our beliefs and expectations determine, to a large extent, how we are affected by events and how we will attempt to deal with them.

It is not unusual for us to adopt fixed and irrational patterns of thinking which limit our ability to respond positively to a problem. We may find it difficult to accept rejection, or we may expect perfection from both ourselves and others. Some common examples of unrealistic thoughts are as follows:

- We typically think that it is important to have approval from everyone, yet occasional rejection or disapproval is inevitable in all relationships, including those at work.

- We typically think that unpleasant events are terrible, yet although a conflict at work is unfortunate and unpleasant, it is rarely, if ever, catastrophic.

- We typically think that people who behave in a way we do not like are bad and should be blamed, yet people will not agree with us all the time.

In addition, we tend to compound the problem by thinking of negative outcomes rather than looking for positive solutions to the conflict. A typical chain of thoughts following a difficult interaction might take the form of: 'Why did they behave like that?'; 'Why me?'; 'If I confront them I will only be the loser'; 'I'm not sure how I can remain working in this situation'.

As a result, we feel less able to control the situation, our confidence in our ability to perform competently diminishes and our self-esteem decreases. Clearly then, our pattern of perceiving and responding to conflict plays an important part in determining whether the outcome is positive or negative. Subsequent chapters deal with how to replace irrational and negative patterns of thinking with more rational and positive ways of thinking.

THREE CASE STUDIES

The following examples illustrate the factors involved in interpersonal conflict and can be used in conjunction with Exercise 1.

❏ *Tom and David are both teachers in their late twenties. They have similar qualifications and work status. They have been working in the same department for almost a year and, as their work overlaps, they share responsibility for particular tasks. Tom is always at work well before the pupils arrive and often works on into the early evening. David, on the other hand, arrives at work just before school starts and leaves shortly after the end of the school day. Tom feels that he is having to take an unfair share of the workload and is preparing to confront David about what he describes as David's 'attitude'.*

▶ This example has all the ingredients of a conflict in the making and illustrates a number of the issues relating to why conflicts arise. In Tom's view, David is not adhering to the fundamental rules of relationships for co-workers as he is not taking his fair share of the workload. There are also elements of a personality clash as Tom appears to be more conscientious in his approach, while David is rather more 'laid back'. It is possible that Tom's and David's perceptions of the situation differ. Indeed, their actual workloads may be similar; David may be more efficient or may take work home with him – differing working practices may generate the appearance of a workload imbalance. In fact, it is possible that David is unaware of the impending confrontation. It is always easier to see things from our own point of view than to perceive events from someone else's perspective. If in doubt, simply try to sit down with the other person and tell them how you feel at the earliest possible stage. Negative feelings generated by differing perceptions of the same situation may simmer unnecessarily until they result in open conflict.

❑ *Sheila is a police officer who is working in a largely male environment where informal relations are well established. Because the group socializes outside work and know each other well, they tend to communicate in ways which may be unclear to people outside the group. As a result, misunderstandings between the group and their female colleague occur regularly. Sheila feels that this has made it difficult for her to be one of the team and has become increasingly isolated, socializing with female colleagues outside her immediate working group. Recently, the problem has been eased somewhat as a another woman has been brought into the team; both women now join their male colleagues for an after work drink.*

▶ This example illustrates the nature of working groups in general and the affect that gender-related concerns may have. The formation of cliques is almost inevitable in any large organization; it becomes problematic, however, when one, or a very small number, of work colleagues feel excluded because of differing interests or personal characteristics. Sheila, as the sole woman in a largely male environment, felt under pressure to 'be one of the boys' or risk being excluded. In fact, she felt she was treated with more reserve when she socialized with female colleagues outside the group. She was, however, surprised at how rapidly she was assimilated once she began socializing with her male colleagues.

❏ *Ray is a 30-year-old therapist who has been treating a 28-year-old single mother of two young children over a period of a year. Initially a series of weekly sessions was established, although after a few weeks the client began telephoning the clinic to speak to Ray between sessions. At first, Ray did not seek to discourage this contact, and the telephone calls increased in frequency, as did the requests for further appointments. The client also made attempts to obtain Ray's home telephone number from the clinic's secretarial staff. Although Ray felt that her condition had improved substantially, the client denied any improvement and insisted that Ray would be able to help her. Indeed, Ray attempted to terminate treatment at one stage but was persuaded to continue when told, 'I will not be able to cope without your help'. Ray began to dread the telephone calls and appointments although he has gradually decreased the frequency of both.*

▶ Two important aspects of interpersonal conflict are illustrated here: the breaking of relationship rules and manipulation of the professional–client relationship. The client ignored the boundaries of the professional relationship by repeated telephone calls and by trying to contact the therapist at home. She tried to manipulate the relationship by vesting Ray with responsibility for her condition, alternately making him feel guilty for not helping her and, at the same time, assuring him that he was the only one who could help her (see Chapter 4). The client has to be told at an early stage that no therapist has all the answers and that there are limitations on each client's time with the therapist. This is not necessarily an easy matter. However, it is only by clearly establishing the limits and boundaries of relationships that later conflict can be avoided.

CONFLICT ANALYSIS

The following framework is a useful guide for the anlysis of any interpersonal conflict. Aspects to consider are its history, its context, other interested parties, the issues involved and its dynamics.

☐ *Conflict history.* Understanding how a conflict developed can help us to unravel how we came to the present impasse. Ask yourself: 'How did it originally arise?'; 'Did a particular event signal the start of the conflict?'; 'How long has it lasted?'; 'How has it changed over time?'.

☐ *Conflict context.* Examining the context or setting within which the conflict occurs can help us to judge the parameters and extent of the conflict. Ask yourself: 'Does this person have problems with anyone except me?'; 'What behaviours or actions characterize the conflict?'.

☐ *Other interested parties*. Although two people may be in conflict, it is important to place this in a broader organizational or social context. Ask yourself: 'Is anyone fuelling the conflict?'; 'Who will gain if the conflict develops?'.

☐ *Conflict issues*. In resolving a conflict, it is important to identify any specific points of disagreement. Ask yourself: 'Are there any particular facts we disagree about?'; 'Do we have different beliefs about key issues?'; 'Is one or both of us trying to hold on to something (for example, power, free time, incentives)?'; 'Do we have problems communicating?'.

☐ *Conflict dynamics*. No conflict is static; they develop and change over time. Establishing how the conflict has evolved may help to find a way to resolve it. Ask yourself: 'Is the original reason for the conflict the same as it is now or has it changed?'; 'Have our relative positions become more polarized?'; 'Has there been an increase in hostility since the conflict began?'.

The first step in dealing with conflicts at work is thus to understand why they arise and how they subsequently develop. As noted earlier, however, conflicts at work are not unusual and some minor conflicts can be passed over and forgotten. It is therefore necessary to assess which conflicts to deal with and which ones to ignore.

CONFRONTING CONFLICTS – THE COSTS AND BENEFITS

There are five factors, apart from the perceived importance of the conflict, which need to be considered in weighing up the costs and benefits of ignoring or confronting a conflict: the transaction costs, the likely outcome, the effect upon work colleagues and the work environment, the effect upon the relationship and the likelihood of conflict recurrence.

Transaction costs. Confronting a conflict clearly demands a great deal of emotional energy and involves a frustrating amount of time which could be spent on more useful and enjoyable tasks. Questions to ask oneself are: 'If the conflict persists, is this more emotionally draining than if I confront it?'; 'Will I spend more time dwelling on the conflict than if I confront it?'; 'Will my nerves be more "frayed" if I deal with the problem or if I leave it as it is?'.

Likely outcome. It is impossible to know with any degree of certainty the likely outcome of a conflict although there can be only four possible solutions: either party can win, both parties can win or both can lose. Even if the outcome does not entirely fulfil one person's interests, if it is perceived as being fair, a satisfactory resolution is possible. A postive outcome is clearly more likely if both parties feel their views will be heard, if they feel responsible for shaping any settlement, and if they both feel that any third party involved will act fairly. Questions to ask oneself are: 'Will I have the opportunity to say what I think?'; 'Will the other party be receptive to my viewpoint?'. 'Is any third party involved completely neutral?'. We might even ask ourselves: 'Is any outcome better than the continuance of the conflict?'.

The effect upon work colleagues and the work environment. When confronting a conflict at work, it is clearly important to weigh up the broader work-related issues. While a conflict may be between two people, it is rarely possible for others to remain uninvolved. For example, colleagues may side with one or other of the protagonists or may view one of them as being a trouble-maker. Questions to ask oneself are: 'How is the conflict likely to be viewed by work colleagues?'; 'Will I be able to remain in the same work environment if I confront the conflict but the resolution attempt fails?'.

The effect upon the relationship. A desire for an improved long-term working relationship is no doubt one reason for confronting a conflict. Again, it is impossible to tell in advance whether such an aim can be achieved. The involvement of a third party can help the protagonists focus upon appropriate issues and facilitate a relationship in which parties can work together on a day-to-day basis. Questions to ask oneself are: 'Could our working relation-ship deteriorate further?'; 'Could the involvement of a third party in any discussion help us to work together more effectively?'.

EXPLORING REASONS FOR INTERPERSONAL CONFLICTS

EXERCISE 1

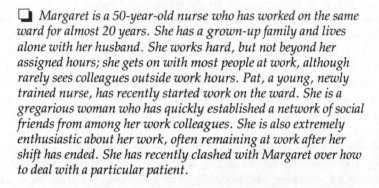

❏ *Margaret is a 50-year-old nurse who has worked on the same ward for almost 20 years. She has a grown-up family and lives alone with her husband. She works hard, but not beyond her assigned hours; she gets on with most people at work, although rarely sees colleagues outside work hours. Pat, a young, newly trained nurse, has recently started work on the ward. She is a gregarious woman who has quickly established a network of social friends from among her work colleagues. She is also extremely enthusiastic about her work, often remaining at work after her shift has ended. She has recently clashed with Margaret over how to deal with a particular patient.*

❏ *Tom is a young, ambitious man who joined his current firm two years ago. Although he has no formal qualifications, he has quickly worked his way up to his present position and expects further promotion soon. He socializes with a small group of male colleagues. Ruth, a graduate of similar age to Tom, has recently joined the firm to work in a similar capacity. She is a quietly efficient and instantly likeable young woman. Tom rarely talks to her, avoiding her during formal work-related activities. He has also withheld information from her and made derogatory sexist remarks about her during meetings.*

For both excerpts, consider each of the following questions:

1. What part do you think the pattern of work relationships and friendships plays in the development of each conflict?

2. Is there any indication that one party is generally disliked, or is the conflict specific to the two parties concerned?

3. Have any relationship rules been broken?

4. What contribution do you think age or gender differences make in each situation?

5. How do you think each person perceives the situation?

The likelihood of conflict recurrence. A resolution which does not endure is likely to intensify the original conflict. Factors which increase the likelihood of a satisfactory outcome to the conflict are those that are likely to diminish the possibility of conflict recurrence. It is important to be mindful of situations where the conflict between two parties is resolved, but is then pursued with someone else. For example, a person guilty of sexual harassment may refrain from harassing someone who has confronted them, but may continue to harass someone else instead. In this regard, it is important to ask ourselves whether the conflict is restricted to the two parties involved or whether it is part of a more general pattern of behaviour.

Although there will inevitably be some costs involved in confronting a conflict, these are likely to be offset by the benefits of an improved working relationship. In weighing up the costs and benefits, a judgement of high costs is likely to mean that the conflict will not be addressed. It is important to remember that some factors can be dealt with more readily than others. It is easier to understand our own behaviour and perceptions of events and to modify these, than it is to change someone else's behaviour. Nevertheless, modifying our own behaviour can serve to influence the attitudes and reactions of those with whom we work.

Chapter Two

The Difficult Boss

Most of us are accountable to someone else at work. This may be via clear routes, for example, a class teacher is accountable to the headteacher, a police officer is accountable to the sergeant, a ward nurse is accountable to the charge nurse and so on. More senior people in organizations are also accountable to others, although this may be to groups such as school governors or government departments, rather than to individuals. Senior personnel in any hierarchy are thus at the interface between those they manage and those to whom they are accountable. As such they are constrained from above, although the degree of constraint will vary between organizations depending on the extent to which the person or group with overall authority actually exercises their control. Thus a strong school governing body may have considerable influence over a headteacher's actions; decisions taken by a health service manager or a chief constable may directly affect the managerial capacity of a charge nurse or police sergeant. Within such constraints, however, the exercise of power by one person over another within a work environment is influenced by two main factors, namely, managers' perceptions of their responsibilities and the rules of superior–subordinate relationships.

Expectations about what a manager or boss should do. The many roles a manager fulfils may vary between organizations, although it is possible to recognize common factors. If the manager's role is clearly delineated, it becomes easier to define responsibilities and delegate tasks to those in the manager's charge, and to establish appropriate channels of communication. Conversely, an organization in which there is little role definition, will hinder even the most skilled manager. The priority assigned to different roles will be influenced and constrained both by the nature of the organization and, more implicitly, its function, as well as by the general managerial style of the person concerned.

Rules of superior–subordinate relationships. Even if roles are clearly defined, clumsy or inappropriate treatment of others or behaviour which breaks the rules of superior–subordinate relationships can detract from the advantages of a well-structured organization. Although there are clearly differences in the way people manage others, management inevitably involves the exercising of power over others. If used appropriately, power can be used to facilitate good working practices and to enhance job satisfaction; when used inappropriately, however, it can generate hostility and conflict.

BEING A MANAGER

The interrelated nature of the various roles has led one writer to liken the performance of managers to a symphony orchestra conductor who is 'endeavouring to maintain a melodious performance in which the contributions of the various instruments are co-ordinated and sequenced, patterned and spaced, while the orchestra members are having various personal difficulties, stage hands are moving music stands, alternating excessive heat and cold are creating audience and instrument problems, and the sponsor of the concert is insisting on irrational changes in the programme' (Sayles, 1964). By delineating the various roles involved in managing others, it is possible to identify the set of parameters which result in the least conflict between manager and managed.

MANAGERIAL ROLES

Mintzberg (1973) suggests that managers are responsible for the following range of tasks:

Interpersonal roles
Figurehead:
- Represents the department or organization at official functions and ceremonies, for example, presenting awards, meeting parents or local dignitaries.

Leader:
- Delegates tasks and responsibilities.
- Appoints and dismisses staff.
- Sets goals and steers the organization towards them.

Liaison:
- Maintains good relations both within the organization and with the outside world.
- Encourages participation and good working practices.

Informational roles

Monitor:
- Is aware of what is happening both inside and outside the organization.
- Attends informal and formal meetings.
- Reads internal and external working papers, reports and documents relating to the profession to keep up-to-date. For example, police, health care workers and educators need to be aware of legislative changes, changes in professional practice and current evidence or research which might impinge on their working practice.

Disseminator:
- Creates appropriate channels (newsletters, meetings) for disseminating information effectively within the organization.

Spokesperson:
- Distributes information about the organization and its activities to external bodies.

Decision-making

Entrepreneur:
- Introduces new working practices or reorganizes and restructures existing ones as necessary.
- Formulates specific aims for the department or organization.
- Takes initiatives to improve the work environment.

Disturbance handler:
- Deals with disputes and disagreements.
- Needs keen interpersonal skills.

Resource allocator:
- Makes decisions relating to budgets, allocation of resources and expenditure.

Negotiator:
- Promotes staff and organizational interests, meeting with governors, unions, health service managers, etc.

Clearly, co-ordinating these roles demands much skill, and the way in which managers perceive and carry out their various responsibilities will have a significant effect on their relationships with their subordinates. Tasks such as reorganizing a department, resolving disputes and allocating resources all require a great deal of sensitivity to the needs of others. An open leadership style which encourages communication and participation and which introduces fair decision-making procedures is usually most effective.

MANAGERIAL STYLES

Managing others clearly requires a wide range of skills. A number of theoretical conceptualizations of leadership have been applied to the work environment; some assume that the inherent personal characteristics of the person are all important; others emphasize the importance of individuals' behaviour and the priorities they attach to their role. Some theories have attempted to match various leader characteristics and behaviour to particular tasks. Three dimensions of leadership style have emerged from the research: structuring, supporting and democratic-persuasive leadership.

A *structuring style* is one in which the manager focuses upon the task at hand and its completion. Such a manager is more likely to be directive, primarily concerned with work procedures and time deadlines.

A *supporting style* involves a concern for people and the development of their capabilities. A supportive manager is thus more likely to focus on maintaining good relationships within the working group. The suitability of different combinations of structuring and supporting styles in relation to particular tasks and work environments has been investigated and the results have formed the basis of managerial training programmes. Some have suggested that a structuring style is associated with greater work output, while a supporting style is associated with greater work satisfaction. However, this association is far from clear-cut and is likely to be influenced by a range of factors, including the particular work environment, the demands of the task and the characteristics of the co-workers and managers involved.

A *democratic-persuasive style* uses both participation and persuasion so that it is possible to deal with the task at hand and any interpersonal concerns at the same time. A key element of this style is that of flexibility – the ability to ascertain when a structuring style and when a supporting style is appropriate.

RELATIONSHIP RULES FOR MANAGERS

While the delineation of managerial roles indicates what is expected of a leader, relationship rules facilitate the effective operationalization of these roles. As with any relationship, the relationship between supervisor and supervisee is an interactive process with rules governing the behaviour of both.

RULES FOR SUPERIORS

▶ Keep subordinates informed and/or consult them about decisions which are likely to affect them.

▶ Advise and encourage subordinates and facilitate their advancement.

▶ Assign work fairly and with explanation.

▶ Show understanding for subordinates' personal problems.

▶ Stand up for subordinates' interests as necessary.

RULES FOR SUBORDINATES

☐ Follow reasonable orders, but do not be too submissive. It is acceptable to question orders which are unclear.

☐ Follow instructions but use initiative when appropriate.

☐ Put forward and defend one's own ideas when appropriate.

☐ Direct complaints through the immediate superior rather than to others.

☐ Accept constructive criticism.

RULES FOR SUPERIORS AND SUBORDINATES

• Respect each other's privacy.

• Do not talk about the other person behind their back.

• Do not pay unannounced social calls.

• Avoid sexual activity between superior and subordinate.

A breakdown of supervisor–supervisee relationship rules is a major source of conflict. Unfair treatment or lack of consultation or encouragement is likely to result in decreased job satisfaction which may, in turn, have a negative effect upon health and well-being. Conversely, a manager who combines the 'right amount' of consideration for subordinates with the 'right amount' of instruction, training, checking, correcting and motivating, is likely to engender high job satisfaction. The problem for the manager is possessing both the will and the ability to gauge what the right amount actually is.

POWER

The manager or supervisor inevitably has power purely by virtue of his or her position within the organization. No matter what the manager's personal characteristics are, he or she is in a position to control the behaviour of others. It is possible to identify five ways in which such power can operate in superior–subordinate relationships. These are reward, coercive, expert, legitimate and referent power.

Reward power. As noted, a superior should offer tangible rewards such as financial incentives or promotion. Perhaps even more important is the day-to-day use of praise or encouragement. A metaphorical pat on the back, saying 'thank you' or 'well done' is a simple but sadly neglected way of making people feel valued for their efforts and can go a long way towards encouraging harmony at work.

Coercive power. It is not unusual for either threat and/or praise to be used to enforce a particular behaviour even though the subordinate may not wish to comply. This may take the form of comments such as, 'Well, if you don't want to do this job I can always find something less pleasant for you', or, 'You may feel that this isn't the job for you, but you know you are the only one I can trust to do it properly'. Being pushed into a task or role which one would rather not perform, invariably provides fertile ground for resentment.

Expert power. This is characteristic of professional relationships where knowledge and skill place one person in a position of authority. Such a person can provide information, as in the teacher–pupil relationship, or help and guidance, as in doctor–patient or social worker–client relationships. Clearly expert power can also be exercised within supervisor–supervisee relationships.

The authority of the supervisor depends not only on their knowledge and skill, but also on the respect and acknowledgement of the supervisee. Advice or information from a superior whose expertise we doubt or do not value is unlikely to change our behaviour.

Legitimate power. This refers to the exercise of power by virtue of one person's acceptance of the other's authority. This is more usually based on their relative positions within a work hierarchy than on specific knowledge or skills. However, acceptance of another's authority is often based on some degree of respect for that person, which may involve a recognition of their experience, knowledge or expertise.

Referent power. This refers to the vesting of power in another person because we admire them. Supervisees might try to imitate supervisors if the latter are sufficiently admired – either because of their success and achievements or because of their capacity to reward the supervisee.

THE CONSEQUENCES OF POWER

The five forms of power can fall into two main groups: reward and coercive power rely upon sanctions; expert and referent power rely upon mutual respect and compliance. Legitimate power is based on subordinates accepting the authority of those who are more powerful, and can fall into either of these groups depending on whether or not sanctions are used. The use of power can have destructive, productive or integrative consequences.

Power can be destructive if it involves excessive reliance on sanctions to control others. This may result in submission, defiance, counterthreat or complete withdrawal. Clearly, defiance and counterthreat are inherent ingredients of conflict. Misuse of legitimate power or excessive use of coercive power is potentially destructive and likely to lead to the development of conflict.

Productive power, on the other hand, involves an element of reciprocity. This may take the form of reward in return for good performance, or co-operation in working practice in return for involvement in decision-making. The development of productive working practices is likely to be associated with appropriate use of reward and legitimate power.

Integrative power is based upon respect which goes beyond the mere exchange involved in productive power. Integrative power results from the capacity to inspire loyalty and a common sense of purpose for people working in an organization. Integrative power is most likely to involve an effective combination of reward, legitimate and expert power.

GENDER AND POWER

Women in managerial or supervisory positions may experience special difficulties in their relationships at work if their male colleagues or subordinates are threatened by them. A survey conducted in the United States in the 1960s found that more than two-thirds of men and almost one-fifth of women would feel uncomfortable working for a female boss. A similar picture emergd in a further US survey conducted a decade later. It might be assumed that the 'threatened male syndrome' might decrease as more women enter employment and occupy positions of authority. However, one report found that although male resistance to female managers decreased as more women were appointed, when the ratio of male to female managers fell to below ten to two, a rapid increase in resistance occurred; presumably because the number of women, rather than women per se, was perceived as threatening.

Working women may also be affected by the commonly held assumption that men are more likely to be task-orientated, objective and independent and therefore more suited to handling managerial responsibilities. Women, who are viewed as being more passive and submissive, would be regarded as less suited to higher positions. It is also frequently assumed that women managers are more considerate than their male counterparts. Indeed, in this regard, there is some evidence that women managers are likely to score higher on the supporting dimension of leadership attributes than male colleagues. Overall, though, there is little evidence to suggest that there are any substantive gender differences in leadership style. However, because of the tendency for women to show a greater concern for relationships, some argue that women are more suitable than men as managers.

Despite many changes, men still predominate in high status positions. Because of the inherent power associated with such positions, opportunities exist for abuse – particularly with subordinates who may depend on their managers for promotion or other work-related needs. Extreme instances are cases of sexual harassment: people in higher positions misusing their authority to coerce lower status people into sexual relationships. The harasser uses his position of power both to exhort sexual gratification and to demean the subordinate and maintain his position of power. Clearly such behaviour violates basic relationship rules.

AGE AND POWER

As noted in Chapter 1, knowledge and experience are not necessarily related; younger personnel may be more knowledge-able while older personnel are more experienced. This presents two potential sources of conflict in managing others: the older, experienced manager in charge of younger, but more knowledge-able, personnel or, conversely, a younger, more knowledgeable manager in charge of older, more experienced personnel. Although in both instances the manager possesses legitimate power, the extent to which they can rely on either expert or referent power is restricted by the supervisee's claim to either greater knowledge or greater skill. This may pose a particular problem for the younger manager – length of service in any organization still merits some respect, so that age and experience are likely to be greater assets than knowledge and youth. In such instances, the young person's inexperience may lead to an excessive reliance on the destructive use of reward and coercive power to control others. It is important for the younger manager to work hard to gain the respect and acknowledgement of others. Referent power can be increased by being considerate to staff members, treating them fairly and defending their interests to higher management. Expert power can be established by cultivating an image of competence, even in the absence of experience per se; appearing to be confused, vacillating or panicking will quickly diminish expert power.

CONFLICT WITH MANAGERS

Studies examining the relationship between managers and those they manage show that recognizing, acknowledging and considering the needs of others results in a considerable reduction in job pressure. Mutual trust, respect and a certain degree of warmth epitomize such relationships. Conversely, leaders who show favouritism, criticize unnecessarily, who pull rank or who take undue advantage of their positions, create an environment in which hostility and tension predominate.

Not adhering to the informal rules of the relationship; knowing the rules but not exhibiting the appropriate skills; adopting a leadership style which is inappropriate to the demands of the situation; or abusing the power of one's position are common causes of conflict in the workplace. To some extent these factors are interactive: inappropriate leadership style or non-adherence to relationship rules are more likely when the person concerned lacks the necessary management skills.

MISUSING POWER

The famous saying of Lord Acton that power tends to corrupt and absolute power corrupts absolutely holds credence at all levels of society. But why do people misuse legitimate power or make excessive use of coercive power?

People with an excessive need or desire to exert control over others may misuse legitimate power. This may occur either because of their inherent insecurity or because of a misguided drive for control. As Judith, a clinical psychologist, comments:

❑ *For the first three years in her post, my immediate superior was the only member of the department. She was promoted very rapidly, partly because of the absence of any competition. As more staff have been appointed, she has become more and more defensive and wants to have control over even the most trivial decisions. It seems as if we are unable to do anything without asking her first – it is creating a most unpleasant working environment.*

People who have illusions of power are also likely to abuse legitimate power, or use coercive power excessively. Such people believe that their status is greater than it is in reality, and may attempt to exert control when it is not entirely appropriate to do so. As Chris, a teacher, comments:

❑ *The head of my department seems to think he runs the school. Although he has a perfect right to run his department as he sees fit, some of his decisions run counter to the school's policy. He puts you in a difficult position though, because you know he will go out of his way to help you if you agree with him.*

People who feel powerless or threatened may use coercive power excessively in an attempt to establish an assumed level of power. As Andrew, a policeman, comments:

❑ *My sergeant seems to go out of his way to make our lives difficult; he's always threatening us over something. I'm sure its partly because he's made to feel useless himself; most decisions are made by his own superiors so he takes it out on us.*

A manager's behaviour will clearly reflect his or her attitude to power. An excessive need to exert control may manifest itself in an inability to encourage others to take responsibility, by not allowing them to take the lead or by withholding information from them. Coercive power may operate through the favoured allocation of resources or promotion prospects for those least likely to threaten the manager's own power. Rather than negotiating, decisions are likely to be imposed; rather than seeking to settle disturbances, disagreements may be encouraged in order to meet the manager's own needs. The rules which govern behaviour between superior and subordinate are also transgressed. A subordinate's behaviour may be criticized publicly, confidences may be broken, and they may be treated unfairly. Although power can be misused in fairly obvious ways, for example, withholding information or imposing decisions, power can also be misused in more insidious ways in the form of 'put-downs'.

PUT-DOWNS

Put-downs can take many forms, ranging from personal attacks which are overt and aggressive, to everyday put-downs which are more subtle but perhaps more insidious. By their very nature, personal attacks are not directed at resolving issues but are aimed at the individuals themselves. The following are typical examples:

'You really need to be aware of the facts – you should know that that's not the case.'
'I can't imagine what possessed you to suggest such an idea!'
'That's quite untrue and you've been here long enough to know it!'

Both personal attacks and put-downs frequently occur rapidly and out of the blue, their unexpected nature sometimes leaving the victim flustered and speechless. A single put-down is unlikely to engender anything other than mild annoyance. However, if they occur with any degree of frequency and are not dealt with, they are likely to fester and grow. They may eventually become an established part of an interaction, slowly souring one's relationship with the instigator. Such put-downs can cause particular frustration and anger if they occur in meetings or in front of others and can take various forms.

Ignoring. If someone ignores our comments or statements, this can serve as a powerful put-down; talking through or interrupting our attempts to offer input and ideas, or making decisions on our behalf works in a similar way.

Sarcasm. This can either be implied by tone of voice or conveyed by the use of 'clever' and cutting comments. Comments such as, 'What a wonderful idea' or 'Only you could have thought of something like that' can be readily turned, by subtle changes of tone, into damning put-downs.

Blaming. This can take the form of exaggerating genuine mistakes or missed deadlines, or simply implying fault where none exists. Comments such as, 'If only you'd looked at the notes' or 'You should check these things before meetings' can be especially hurtful, particularly if they are voiced in front of valued colleagues.

Dismissing. This can take the form of dismissive hand gestures, or facial expressions such as sneers which demean suggestions. Verbal comments such as, 'That clearly won't work' or 'We'll need a better idea than that' act in a similar way.

Patronizing. Being treated condescendingly is also a powerful put-down. Typical comments might include, 'Well that wasn't so difficult was it?' or 'If you don't think you're up to it I'll have to do it myself'.

The following case study illustrates how powerful put-downs can be:

❏ *Andy is a 39-year-old lecturer with many years of teaching and research experience. He is currently working as a hospital researcher. He was appointed to his previous job, working in a university, approximately two years ago. He was given a three year contract and was responsible for setting up and running a new course. He was directly accountable to the head of department (called 'M' for present purposes), a man of similar age who was, if anything, slightly less qualified than Andy. At first everything seemed to run smoothly, with Andy left, for the most part, to his own devices. Gradually, and quite subtly, the picture began to change. At meetings attended by both men, Andy would be contradicted by 'M' and his authority questioned. 'M' began to make his own arrangements with teaching staff concerning their contribution to Andy's course. These arrangements often didn't match the way the course was actually*

*organized, leading to disagreements between Andy and other members of
the department. Allocation of resources was often delayed and certain
information essential for the smooth running of the course was withheld.
The occurrence of put-downs increased, with Andy frequently being
ignored, blamed or patronized during meetings and in the presence of other
members of staff. Andy also heard that 'M' described him as 'useless' to
other members of the department. Finally, 'M' began collecting draft
minutes of meetings from Andy's secretary and altering them without
discussion. Although his position became increasingly untenable, Andy
felt unable to address the situation because he was afraid that his three year
contract would not be renewed. He tried to manage in spite of the
difficulties, attempting to remain polite and courteous at all times. As a
consequence, his health began to suffer, he had increasing difficulty
sleeping and was often ill. Eventually Andy found his current hospital post
and resigned from his university job with one year of his three year contract
still remaining.*

▶ How could Andy have managed the situation? It could be
argued that he displayed the ultimate use of power by resigning
and selling his skills to another organization. However, an
intolerable situation had developed which Andy had endured for a
considerable period of time, and both his self-confidence and
health had suffered. Andy tolerated unjustified criticism and put-
downs and made little attempt to deal with them, either at the time
or later in private consultation with 'M'. This lack of action might
have actually served to increase 'M's' behaviour. It is important to
respond to unwarranted criticism and put-downs immediately.

DEALING WITH PUT-DOWNS

No doubt we have all received criticism which we felt was
unjustified or which was stated in the form of a put-down. No
doubt we have also responded to such situations either with an
inappropriate display of aggression or by remaining quiet while
seething inside, feeling angry for some time afterwards. Our
interpretation of the criticism clearly plays a large part in
determining how we respond. We may validate the criticism, even
if it is unjustified, by looking for possible failings in ourselves. A
typical self-blaming thought might be, 'Oh no, I always seem to be
doing things wrong'. Conversely, we may always find fault with
the other person. A typical other-blaming thought might be, 'They
always seem to find something wrong'. Such extremes inevitably

lead to avoidance or aggression. It is unlikely that we 'always' make mistakes and it is unlikely that other people 'always' criticize our actions. If you do not agree with the criticism or feel that you have been put down, made to feel small or criticized in front of colleagues, remember you have the right to say so.

The easiest way of dealing with a put-down or unjustified criticism is to let it pass. Alternatively, one can respond with an equally 'clever' retort. Neither of these ways of dealing with a put-down is likely to reduce their frequency. Indeed, an increase in such behaviour may result, either because the person receives no sanction for their behaviour, or because they may actually enjoy niggling you or making you feel uncomfortable. In dealing with a put-down, it is important to remain calm, to stand up for yourself and to feel good about it afterwards. Three main steps can be identified: preparing, challenging and standing up for oneself.

1. *Preparing.* The initial step involves literally taking a deep breath and preparing yourself psychologically, thinking realistically and positively. As mentioned, put-downs can often occur out of the blue, giving you too little time to think. As with Andy's case, however, they are seldom one-offs, but are rather an established part of interacting. This makes their occurrence almost predictable, allowing you more time to prepare yourself.

2. *Challenging.* The second step involves using set phrases or questions which demand a response from the other person and which give you more time to think how to proceed. If you feel that you have been criticized unjustly, you can ask for clarification or possible examples of your mistake. Such a request should not be offered as a challenge to the person's integrity, but simply as an assertive challenge of your right to know. Typical challenges include the following:

- *Seeking information*: 'Can you give me some examples of what you mean?'.

- *Asking for clarification*: 'Why did you say that?' or 'What do you mean by . . . ?'.

- *Checking your understanding*: 'Have I got this right? Am I to assume you mean . . . '.

3. *Standing up for oneself.* The third step may begin with a brief and to the point statement which asserts your position. If a put-down or criticism is made in the form of a personal attack, try to separate

the personal nature of the remark from the actions criticized. There may be some validity to the content of the criticism, even if it was stated inappropriately. If that is the case, try to acknowledge its validity to your boss, but make it clear that you would prefer it not to be delivered in the form of a personal attack. The following are typical assertive responses.

Put-down	Assertive response
Ignoring	Re-statement of one's position, perhaps prefaced by a comment such as: 'I'm sorry, but I think this is an important point . . . '.
Sarcasm 'What a wonderful idea'	'Wonderful might be too strong a word, but it is certainly an idea that I think merits further discussion'.
Blaming 'If only you'd looked at the notes'	'I accept that I could have checked beforehand, but it is unlikely that it would have changed my views on the matter'.
Dismissing 'That clearly won't work'	'I believe it will work and perhaps we should discuss it or give it a trial run'.
Patronizing 'If you don't think you're up to it I'll have to do it'	'I do think I'm up to it and I'm quite happy to look after it myself'.

Clearly, these three steps serve only as a guide and should be used flexibly. It may be necessary to offer more than one challenge or you may be able to state where you stand immediately. It is important to remain calm and appear positive. Hopefully, the occurrence of put-downs will decrease but, if someone is determined to misuse their power, then put-downs may continue. As mentioned, however, the aim is to feel good about yourself afterwards and to maintain your feelings of self-confidence and self-esteem. Should put-downs persist, it is important to remember that they do not reflect your behaviour or capabilities, a fact which will gradually become obvious to everyone who has witnessed your altercations with the boss. Assertive responses will be respected and your superior will eventually lose face in the eyes of the staff.

RECEIVING CONSTRUCTIVE CRITICISM

Criticism which is unjustified or phrased in the form of a put-down clearly differs from constructive criticism. While the former is said with a deliberate intent to hurt, the latter is intended to be helpful. Constructive criticism should involve the provision of accurate feedback stated in a calm and rational manner. Although there may be occasions when such feedback is stated tactlessly, the context in which the feedback occurs and our knowledge of the person providing it, should lead us to a correct judgement of its intent. However, the way we react to such criticism will largely be determined by how we perceive and assess it. If we feel that the criticism is indeed directed towards us personally rather than being a constructive comment on our performance or behaviour, we may well interpret it as a put-down. There are a number of steps we can take to ensure that we have interpreted the criticism accurately and that we respond appropriately.

Initially we may offer the same challenges as for put-downs; that is seeking information, asking for clarification and checking understanding. Answers to these questions will give a clearer idea of whether we have interpreted the situation accurately. Having established that the criticism was intended to be helpful, the next step is to consider our own feelings about receiving criticism. If our typical reaction is, 'Any criticism is bad', or 'I should not make mistakes', then we are likely to feel threatened – even by comments which are intended to be helpful. If, after thinking about it, we still do not accept the criticism as being appropriate, then it is important to say so. If, however, we recognize that the criticism is genuinely justified, we should be able to use it to our advantage; we might even thank the person for helping to point out problems which we can subsequently correct.

ACKNOWLEDGING PERSONAL POWER

Power has been referred to as a means by which one individual can control another. At another level, however, power refers to our own personal ability to control our lives, to value ourselves and to

COPING WITH PUT-DOWNS

'Even you can manage that' is an example of a put-down to which one can respond: 'I have no doubt I can manage it; I manage far more complex tasks than this'.

1. Think of responses to the following put-downs:

    'Given the amount of time you seem to have, I would have expected better of you.'

    ....
    ....
    ....

    'That's typical of you.'

    ....
    ....
    ....

    'You know that's irrelevant to the discussion.'

    ....
    ....
    ....

2. Add to the list with put-downs you have experienced in the past.

    ....
    ....
    ....

3. How could you have responded to these comments?

    ....
    ....
    ....

4. Take action in real life, but remember to prepare yourself and offer a challenge if the put-down occurs 'out of the blue'.

    ....
    ....
    ....
    ....

make choices. Personal power involves a sense of self-worth, an ability to have insight into others as well as an ability to deal with the world around us, even when it is threatening. While power as control can serve to generate conflict, personal power gives us control of our own lives so that we can take steps to address conflicts which occur. Unfortunately, while we often view others as powerful, we frequently view ourselves as being relatively powerless. Certainly, in the earlier example, Andy felt increasingly devalued and powerless to change the situation; his own feelings of personal power were devalued until the only way he felt able to exert control was by resigning from his job. He could have asserted his personal power earlier by deciding to question and stand up for his rights. Although the legitimate power may rest with someone else, each of us has the ultimate power to take decisions about how we want to control our lives. However, the use of personal power is often impeded by self-imposed barriers to action. These barriers often involve unrealistic expectations we have of ourselves such as:

I must always be liked.
I must always be nice.
I must never appear vulnerable.
I must never show my feelings.
I must never make or admit to a mistake.
I will never be able to handle rejection or criticism.

Self-statements such as these are not unusual but, in using them, we place ourselves in an impossible situation. These assertions cannot always be true – it is impossible to always be liked and never to appear vulnerable. The more we hold such absolute views, the less likely it is that we will seek to use our personal power. The first step in using personal power thus involves acknowledging that we cannot always be liked, that we will sometimes show our feelings, make mistakes or appear vulnerable. Replace *always* with *sometimes* and *never* with *occasionally*.

RECOGNIZING BARRIERS TO ACTION

There are two internal barriers to action – our habitual ways of thinking and our feelings. The former may take the form of an inner dialogue, in which we articulate thoughts which are often negative and unrealistic. It is important to recognize our pattern of thinking, to evaluate how realistic these thoughts are and to replace them with more realistic and helpful alternatives. Our negative thoughts are closely related to the tendency to feel that, in some way, we must be to blame for the situation and that it is better to remain quiet than to speak out. Removing barriers to action means changing our pattern of thinking and learning to feel confident and assertive.

Negative thoughts might include: 'I missed my chance to reply, but I don't imagine there's anything I could do'. 'Everyone is watching. Why is he trying to show me up?'.

More positive thoughts might include: 'Next time I'll be prepared and will stand up for myself'. 'I must not blame myself; I'm sure others recognize it is his/her problem and not mine'.

Negative thoughts can fall into one of the following categories:

Overgeneralizing. Statements which overlook our positive qualities or successes and dwell on the negative or turn us into victims. Typical thoughts might be: 'I seem to get into this sort of situation all the time' or 'Why does he only pick on me?'. Such thoughts are self-defeating; after all, it is unlikely that we get into this sort of situation *all the time* or that he *only* picks on us.

Black-or-white thinking. This includes all-or-nothing statements which fail to recognize that there are possible intermediate actions. Typical thoughts might be: 'It's better to remain quiet or I will lose my job' or 'I will not say anything now but will have my say when the time is right'. Remember that both inaction and aggression can increase behaviour which we would like to prevent. Standing up for ourselves is much more likely to lead to the desired results.

Absolutist thinking. These are thoughts which include the words *must, should, always, never.* Typical thoughts include: 'I must always be liked' and 'I must never show my feelings'. It is important to remember that it is impossible for us to be liked by everyone and that appropriately expressing how we feel can sometimes be to our advantage.

Self-blame and inaction are likely to be associated with feelings of helplessness and embarrassment as well as with a degree of frustration and anger. Thinking positively and attempting to take sound action depend on your confidence in your own ability to cope.

RECOGNIZING BARRIERS TO ACTION

Refer back to the example of Andy (see page 34). Think about the mental barriers he imposed to prevent himself taking action.

1. What kinds of negative thoughts do you think he had? Add to these examples:

   'Why is he always picking on me?'.
   'I have to watch what I say or I might lose my job'.
   'There's nothing I can do to change things'.

   ....
   ....
   ....
   ....
   ....
   ....
   ....

2. Replace each negative thought with a more positive thought, for example, 'Next time he picks on me I will point out to him what he is doing'.

   ....
   ....
   ....
   ....
   ....
   ....
   ....
   ....

LEARN TO USE PERSONAL POWER

Using personal power involves standing up for your rights without violating those of others. You need to be able to express your beliefs, feelings, opinions, wants and needs in an appropriate, direct and honest way. However, acting assertively requires an awareness and understanding of your feelings and thoughts. This involves:

▶ *Thinking realistically.* It is important to recognize how your pattern of thinking might act as a barrier to action.

▶ *Being aware of your thoughts and feelings.* Knowing what to say and do involves being aware of your thoughts, feelings and needs. Exercise 4 is designed to give you some idea of how you perceive yourself. Think carefully about each question and try to be honest with yourself. Remember, however, that your own perception of yourself will not necessarily be the same as someone else's perception. If you wish, you can ask someone who knows you well and whose opinion you trust to complete the exercise, rating their impression of you. Any discrepancies between your ratings and their ratings will give you some idea of the difference between your view of yourself and others' impressions of you.

▶ *Communicating what you want.* It is important to know what you expect of yourself and the situation so that you can take the initiative and state your needs clearly and openly.

▶ *Standing up for yourself.* It is only by telling people what you think and what your limits are that you can prevent them from manipulating you, taking advantage of you or putting you down.

▶ *Using the appropriate amount of strength.* It is important to use just the right amount of 'muscle', being neither too timid nor too aggressive.

Understanding managerial roles and rules of supervisor–supervisee relationships makes it easier to judge what should be expected in such relationships and where responsibility lies for conflict. Remember, however, that even if, in our perception, the fault lies entirely with our boss, responsibility for continuing conflict is shared. Unless we choose to stand up for ourselves, we will become part of a vicious cycle of conflict.

ASSESSING YOURSELF

EXERCISE 4

Rate each of the following statements on the scale: 1 = always
2 = sometimes   3 = rarely   4 = never

Rating

1. I am aware of how I feel. ☐
2. My thoughts about myself are realistic. ☑ 2
3. I think positively about my actions. ☐ 2
4. I can acknowledge my weaknesses and my strengths. ☐
5. I can express my wants and needs. ☐ 2
6. I recognize my own personal power. ☐ 2
7. I can own up to my mistakes. ☐ 2
8. I know when enough is enough. ☐ 1
9. I know when to assert myself. ☐ 2
10. I can handle appropriate criticism. ☐ 2
11. I can be assertive without being aggressive. ☐ 2
12. I know when to stand up for myself. ☐ 1
13. I can speak out against put-downs. ☐ 2
14. I can take the initiative. ☐ 2
15. I can tell other people what I think. ☐ 2

▶ Total your scores for statements 1 to 3 – these refer to your
awareness of your thoughts and feelings.

▶ Total your scores for statements 4 to 7 – these refer to how
clearly you recognize your needs.

▶ Total your scores for questions 8 to 15 – these refer to how
capable you are of stating your position and needs.

If your first total is less than 6, then you are generally aware of your
thoughts and feelings; any total greater than this suggests that this
is an area for you to work on.

If your second total is less than 8, then you are generally able to
recognize your needs; any total greater than this suggests that this
is an area for you to work on.

If your third total is less than 16, then you are generally able to
state your position and needs; any total greater than this suggests
that this is an area for you to work on.

Chapter Three

Difficulties with Colleagues

As seen in Chapter 1, people at work spend a great deal of time with others of similar status. This time may be spent only working, or may include less formal occasions such as lunch breaks, sports and social activities. Occasionally work colleagues become social friends. As noted previously, however, work relationships do not necessarily develop into social friendships and, indeed, do not have to do so in order to be a source of satisfaction and support. Good relationships at work help to reduce work-related stress; conversely, bad relationships at work are themselves a major stressor. But why should we have difficulties with colleagues and how can we attempt to resolve them? Explanations for conflicts with colleagues at work relate to:

- the general pattern of working relationships within organizations;
- the extent to which the balance within a relationship is considered to be mutually acceptable to both parties;
- the extent to which relationship rules for colleagues are adhered to.

PATTERNS OF WORKING RELATIONSHIPS

INTRA-PROFESSIONAL GROUPS

The way in which we relate to and work with others of comparable status to ourselves is influenced by a range of factors. It seems reasonable to assume that we are more likely to interact with people we work alongside, whose offices are close by, who are working on similar tasks or who fulfil similar roles. We are also more likely to interact with and form friendships with colleagues we like and with whom we share common interests. The complex network of relationships that develop means that even when we are engaged in one-to-one interactions, these will be influenced by other people in the work context. Take, as a hypothetical example, the case of Clive and Sally who work well together, but who also work closely with Martin who likes Sally but not Clive. The working relationship between Clive and Sally will inevitably be influenced by Martin, as well as by their interaction with other colleagues. The formation of particular groupings at work is related both to the sharing of particular tasks and to informal contact with work colleagues.

As noted, working relationships are initially established on the basis of formal contact at work, but are then elaborated by various forms of informal contact. In this way, different groupings are formed at work which have an informal status hierarchy distinct from the one which is formally established. The members of these friendship pairs, subgroups or cliques work together and communicate closely with each other, but may reject or react negatively towards outsiders. Indeed, such communication and friendship patterns are often complex and can develop in a variety of ways. Differing interests, working practices, gender, age, etc. all serve to determine likely group membership. Some simple examples of the many permutations that are possible are presented in Figure 1.

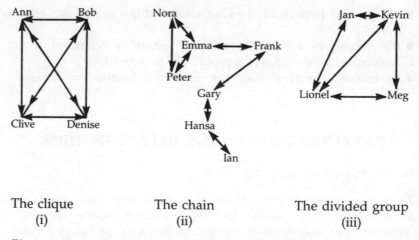

The clique
(i)

The chain
(ii)

The divided group
(iii)

Figure 1. Examples of interaction patterns at work

The clique. The first example illustrates a closed network or clique in which all members of the group relate to each other but not to others outside the group. Although there are likely to be occasional conflicts between group members, conflicts are much more likely to occur if outsiders wish to join the group. Under these circumstances, the clique may operate to form a barrier to change.

The chain. The second example illustrates a chain of people each of whom relates to a different member of the grouping, with one member also relating to another group. Such networks can cause difficulties for a number of reasons. Firstly, some members of the chain may receive information indirectly. For example, information from Frank only reaches Ian via Gary and Hansa. The indirect passing of information inevitably increases the possibility that misunderstandings will occur. Secondly, people often have divided loyalties. For example, Emma will no doubt feel some loyalty to the group containing Nora and Peter, but will also feel loyalty to Frank who is not part of this group. This can have the effect of spreading conflicts because initially disinterested parties can be drawn into disputes.

The divided group. The third example illustrates a network of four people in which there are two subgroups of three people; two group members do not relate directly to each other. Although such structures may occur due to task demands (for example, Jan, Kevin and Lionel may work together on one task and Kevin, Lionel and Meg on another), it would be unusual in a small group for two people to fail to communicate with each other and such a pattern is likely to be illustrative of conflict in the making. Kevin and Lionel, when joined by Jan, may discuss Meg in her absence and, similarly, when joined by Meg, may discuss Jan in her absence. These circumstances may serve to fuel any mistrust Jan and Meg feel for each other.

Anyone who is newly appointed will require time to identify with, and align themselves to, particular groups in an organization. Given that patterns of social and working relationships are already established, conflicts are almost inevitable. Take, for example, the case of Amy, who joins an organization and, finding that she has common interests with one group, gravitates towards it. Amy is well-liked by all the members of the group with the exception of Brian who has been informally identified as group leader. Brian may well feel that his position is under threat and may actively seek to challenge and discredit Amy. Conflict is thus likely to occur when someone is perceived as a threat to an established communication network, friendship or social hierarchy.

INTER-PROFESSIONAL GROUPS

Most working people have a strong allegiance to their own professional group. This intra-professional cohesion is reinforced by shared knowledge, skills and qualifications as well as by profession-specific formal and informal contact such as meetings and training courses. Each profession thus forms a powerful in-group, clinging jealously to what it regards as its own specific knowledge or skill. This can clearly lead to the development of inter-professional conflict rather than co-operation, with each group feeling that they are best equipped to carry out the required duties. Different professions often assume that they have superior skills or knowledge and that they should be the primary decision-makers.

It is not uncommon, particularly within the caring professions, for different professional groups to work closely together. This may be on a relatively informal basis, where there is an assumption that each profession has a relatively unique role, or it may be within the more formalized structure of an interdisciplinary team where professional role boundaries are assumed to be less important. Interdisciplinary teams consisting of social workers, psychologists, psychiatrists and psychiatric nurses are expected to have a primary allegiance to the team, each performing similar duties and each having similar responsibilities. However, anyone who has undergone a long period of professional training, is likely to be more committed to their own professional group than to a team of other professionals, or even to the organization which employs them. Establishing a democratic interdisciplinary group with a freely elected or rotating leadership in which each person is considered of equal status, is no easy matter. Strong adherence to a specific professional identity tends to promote self-interest. Territorial battles and lack of understanding over others' work ethics and styles of working provide fertile ground for many a difficulty.

In an ideal world, inter-professional relationships would be marked by a continuous process of negotiation in which working agreements are created, consolidated or overturned. Unfortunately, the ideal rarely exists; such actions clearly require trust and a spirit of give and take which professional allegiance can mediate against. Resolving inter-professional conflicts involves negotiation and understanding as well as a recognition of the rules governing relationships between colleagues.

RELATIONSHIP RULES FOR COLLEAGUES

Rules for colleagues include:

- Accepting a fair share of the workload.

- Willingness to provide assistance if asked and if the request is reasonable.

- Co-operation with regard to shared space (for example, abide by no-smoking policies, keep coffee areas clean, etc.).

- Working co-operatively with colleagues even if they are people you do not like.

- Respecting each other's privacy.

- Not criticizing a colleague in public.

- Avoiding denigrating a colleague to a superior.

The greatest dissatisfaction in working relationships is created by denigrating a colleague to a superior; in terms of dissatisfaction caused, this is closely followed by criticizing a colleague publicly and failing to accept a fair share of the workload. A fundamental assumption about relationships with colleagues is that they are based on principles of equity and reciprocity. Failure to accept a fair share of the workload or to take responsibility for shared tasks, either because of oversight, laziness or incompetence, constitutes a serious violation of this assumption and can be a major source of conflict in our relationships with colleagues.

RECIPROCAL AND COMPLEMENTARY RELATIONSHIPS

One important aspect of our relationships with others concerns the extent to which they are reciprocal or complementary. Any relationship with an element of dominance–subordinance can be regarded as complementary. One person takes decisions, imparts information and encourages others to work co-operatively. Indeed, because we all have different strengths and weaknesses, interactions which do not involve some element of complementarity are rare. One person may possess more information, be more knowledgeable or have skills pertaining to particular tasks or activities; another may be more capable than another of offering advice or support or may be more resourceful in certain situations.

Working relationships with colleagues can, however, approach a condition of reciprocity. They involve interactions between people of the same status who are engaged in similar tasks. Thus ward nurses work together to complete assigned tasks in a way which facilitates patient care; and police officers, school teachers and social workers work within their respective environments towards common goals. Inevitably, however, working relationships between colleagues are never entirely reciprocal; there is always an element of complementarity. One person may take the lead on some occasions, while a colleague will do so on others.

Factors such as differing degrees of experience may well be appreciated by less experienced colleagues. Indeed, it is common working practice to place experienced and inexperienced colleagues together so that the latter can learn from the former. Similarly, colleagues who have different knowledge or skills may learn from each other in the course of their daily work. The way we relate to colleagues, as with all our relationships, involves a complex interplay of factors and necessitates a degree of give and take. Colleagues of similar status differ in terms of knowledge, skill and experience and there always will be elements of leading and learning in working relationships.

Working relationships can remain harmonious regardless of the extent to which they are reciprocal or complementary if both parties accept the balance. Difficulties arise when one person refuses to share the work or is unable to do so, or assumes a position or status which the other party does not acknowledge or accept. People may presume to have the edge over their colleagues for a variety of reasons. In particular, it is useful to examine how people use common assumptions about age and gender to take on positions of superiority.

AGE DIFFERENCES BETWEEN COLLEAGUES

A person who has spent some time in the same line of work may assume that, because of their experience they 'know best'. This may indeed be the case, and older, more experienced colleagues can often be the best people from whom to learn. As noted in Chapter 1, however, there are occasions when younger employees may well have more up-to-date knowledge or may be better qualified. For example, nursing staff or police officers who entered their professions some years ago are less likely to be university graduates than more recent recruits. However, recent recruits, in turn, may assume they 'know best' because of their greater academic achievements. Clearly, older and younger employees have different skills and knowledge; in an ideal situation, they will acknowledge their relative merits and learn from each other. In order for this to happen, all parties must feel secure with their relative positions and not assume that they automatically 'know best'. Indeed, there are many occasions when a colleague's attempts to dominate are a cover for a deeper sense of insecurity. This can make them difficult people to work with.

GENDER DIFFERENCES BETWEEN COLLEAGUES

Many men still find it difficult to cope with working with women as equals. This is particularly true in male-dominated organizations and is reflected in the way in which women are frequently labelled and categorized at work, so that their status is undermined. It is not uncommon for women to feel that their male colleagues are excessively competitive, or that they create stress and seem to be threatened by them. This reaction seems to increase when women are more competent and competitive. The potential for conflict increases when men strive to maintain their assumed dominance by resorting to put-downs which are blaming ('If only we'd asked X (a male colleague) to do it'), dismissing ('That's typical of a woman') or patronizing ('If you really think a woman could manage . . .'). At worst, men may resort to overly aggressive tactics or sexual harassment to maintain their assumed position of dominance over women in the workplace. This is dealt with further in Chapter 5.

CONFLICT WITH COLLEAGUES

POWER-PLAYS

The concept of power-plays was developed by the American psychologist, Claude Steiner (1981), to describe how people in close relationships attempt to exert control over each other. The concept can also be applied to everyday working relationships with colleagues. A power-play is an attempt to control, exploit and manipulate other people against their will. Power may refer to the extent to which one person's behaviour can be controlled by another (see Chapter 2). However, power between equal status colleagues is, at least in theory, shared evenly. This is true even of complementary relationships where colleagues may have differing roles and experience. If, however, one party wishes to create an imbalance in the relationship against the other's wishes, for example, assume a higher status in an equal status relationship, then they are likely to engage in various power-play strategies. This can remain one-sided, with the protagonist attempting to assert their imagined power over their colleague. In such circumstances, the colleague does not fight back, either because the power-play is ineffective and can be laughed off, or because the person feels defenceless or unable to respond. Alternatively, both parties might vie for power, each resorting to 'unfair fighting tactics' in an attempt to exert control over each other. There is a range of 'unfair fighting tactics' which can include overt threats, psychological threats or game playing.

Overt threats. People use intimidatory physical or verbal threats as power-plays. Although one might assume that most work environments would have enforceable measures to deter threatening behaviour, these frequently prove to be either ineffective or are seldom used. In a recent survey in the United States, some four out of ten women reported suffering some form of sexual harassment while only 15 per cent of them reported it and only five per cent took formal action (US Merit Systems Protection Board, 1988).

Psychological threats. These include a range of more subtle, but equally damaging, 'unfair fighting tactics' intended not only to intimidate the victim but also to manipulate other people's perceptions of him or her. Such tactics include the following:
- attacking a person's emotional weak spots;
- inaccurate reporting about the person to others or telling tales;
- encouraging other people to take the protagonist's side;
- seeking to apportion blame to the other person whenever possible;
- not allowing the person to have their say, either in conversation or in meetings.

Game playing. These strategies involve an element of pretence. Again the aim is to place the protagonist in a good light at the victim's expense. Such tactics include:

- drawing the other person into encounters on false pretences, for example, pretending to be helpful and then sabotaging a task;
- not giving the other person a chance to respond, for example, by making a comment and then leaving the room;
- pretending to be the one who is the victim ('I seem to have lost out here . . .') and then attacking from this vantage point ('If you had not put me into such a difficult position, this never would have happened').

Whether power-plays are one-sided or involve both parties vying for power, energy is focused on winning rather than on solving the problem. One-sided power-plays may be deceptive because no direct conflict is involved. However, particularly when more subtle tactics are used, the victim will be left feeling powerless or resentful as if they have colluded with the protagonist. When two parties vie for power, the interchange is likely to be ongoing without a satisfactory outcome. It is unlikely that one party will accept the needs of the other as legitimate. Fighting back may merely result in more unpleasantness. The only viable options are to choose a middle-ground and attempt to retain your identity and feelings of self-worth, standing up for yourself as appropriate – or to withdraw, either by requesting a transfer to a different work environment within the same organization or by resigning.

❏ *Lucy is 28 years old and has worked for a telecommunications company for just over a year. She works closely with 12 other people of the same status within the organization. She has good working relationships with all her colleagues, with one exception. Betty is a 54-year-old woman who has been employed by the same company for the past seven years. She is generally regarded as a defensive and aggressive person, and her colleagues prefer to stay on her good side. Shortly after joining the company, Lucy formed a friendship with Caroline, one of Betty's closest friends. Initially relations between Lucy and Betty seemed quite cordial but, after a few months, Betty stopped communicating with Lucy who could see no apparent reason for her behaviour. This situation continued for several days until Betty drew Lucy aside, telling her that clearly they had a problem and that she felt Lucy was generally rude and unhelpful. Lucy was taken aback by this reaction as she was unaware of any problems between them and could not recall a situation which could have led Betty to form such an opinion. As a result of the encounter, Lucy became subdued at work, avoiding all contact with Betty when possible. Betty's behaviour gradually became more aggressive. She involved other colleagues in the conflict, attempting to draw them onto her side; Lucy was told by one colleague that Betty had been informing everyone she was forced to have words with Lucy because of Lucy's behaviour. Betty regularly criticized Lucy's work in front of colleagues, and organized social events which she failed to inform Lucy about. Caroline, as a mutual friend of both Betty and Lucy, was placed in a difficult position and attempted to maintain both friendships by working with them on different occasions and socializing with them separately. Eventually Lucy approached the manager to ask for advice about how to handle the situation. Unfortunately, the advice given was, 'Pretend that nothing has happened and carry on as normal'. The problem continues unresolved and Lucy remains in a difficult and unpleasant situation at work.*

Lucy's difficulties illustrate several issues discussed in this chapter. Her presence in the organization challenged an established structure in which Betty regarded herself as informal leader. Although she had no specific knowledge or skills, she maintained this position because no-one wished to antagonize her. Lucy's presence posed a potential threat because, in Betty's eyes, Lucy was drawing away Caroline, her closest ally. Betty made use of a variety of 'unfair fighting tactics' and rule-breaking strategies in an attempt to assert her perceived position as leader. Lucy clearly took the right steps in seeking advice from her manager at this stage. In fact, it transpired that management were aware of the situation and that similar difficulties had arisen between Betty and new employees on previous occasions. Unfortunately the advice offered by management was not particularly useful. As noted above, pretending that unpleasant events have not occurred is inevitably unsatisfactory. Indeed, management could have played a facilitatory role by getting the two parties together in order to address their concerns in the hope that they could negotiate a mutually satisfactory solution. For Lucy, the benefits of confronting the conflict clearly outweighed the costs (see Chapter 1).

DEALING WITH CONFLICT: NEGOTIATING AND BARGAINING

Negotiation shares some characteristics of a 'game of strategy' in which both parties start with different sets of cards which they gradually lay on the table; each party then selects and reselects

POWER-PLAYS AT WORK

EXERCISE 5

Refer to the Lucy case study and consider the following:

1. Lucy became withdrawn at work as a result of Betty's power-plays. Betty used a number of 'unfair fighting tactics' including direct aggression, talking behind Lucy's back and criticizing her in public. How could Lucy have responded to each of these situations in a way which is neither too submissive or aggressive?

....

....

....

....

2. What else could Lucy have done to handle the situation?

....

....

....

....

3. How could management have responded to Lucy's request for advice?

....

....

....

....

cards, weighing up the rewards and costs, until both are satisfied with the new hands they hold. Negotiation, then, is an ongoing process whereby both parties attempt to reach a joint decision about how to define or redefine the terms on which they will 'do business'.

In many ways conflict is an essential part of negotiation – participants put forward differing views which they usually feel strongly about. If, however, both parties recognize the need to achieve a more suitable way of 'doing business', then conflict can be productive rather than destructive. Conflict becomes a means of redefining the situation in terms suitable to both parties rather than an opportunity for one person to control or exert power over another.

I WIN – YOU LOSE

The aim of satisfactory conflict resolution is to involve both parties in mutual problem-solving so that the needs of both are met. Such an outcome has been called a Win–Win solution. When competitive rather than collaborative solutions are sought, it is likely that either the needs of only one party will be met – a Win–Lose situation, or that the needs of neither party will be met – a Lose–Lose situation. There are a range of factors which promote competition rather than collaboration. Indeed, the attempt to resolve a conflict can itself become a power struggle, each person resorting to the power-plays discussed earlier, or repetitively stating their position, becoming increasingly resentful and frustrated. In attempting to resolve a conflict, the manner in which people approach it will play a large part in determining the outcome. Factors which are more likely to promote a Win–Lose or Lose–Lose rather than a Win–Win situation include:

- a belief that one person must lose for the other to win;
- a failure to be entirely open and honest;
- a failure to recognize your own negative points or the other person's positive points;
- engaging in tit-for-tat reactions;
- failing to listen to the other's point of view;
- being too emotive or consistently blaming the other party;
- being too ready to criticize;
- trying to engineer an element of surprise by confronting the situation when one party is unprepared;
- feeling that it is only you who has been misunderstood.

NEGOTIATING WIN–WIN OUTCOMES

There are four steps involved in negotiating acceptable outcomes to conflicts:
Recognizing the existence of a problem.
Understanding each other's position.
Discussing the problem and possible solutions.
Resolving the problem in a mutually acceptable way.

RECOGNIZING THE EXISTENCE OF A PROBLEM

The first phase of conflict resolution involves both parties not only acknowledging that a problem exists, but also agreeing to do something about it. Indeed, some conflicts can be resolved simply by discussing the problem. The majority of instances, however, require the co-operation of the other party in order to engage in active problem-solving. There are four steps involved in recognizing the existence of a problem:

- Acknowledging to yourself that a problem exists.
- Planning the action you will take.
- Alerting the other party to your feelings.
- Enlisting their co-operation in resolving the conflict.

Acknowledging the problem. In order to acknowledge a problem, we have to believe that the benefits of confronting the issue will outweigh the costs. The problem must be perceived as important enough to be acknowledged and we have to feel capable of dealing with any conflict that arises. A victim might find it easier not to 'see' the problem and to retain the status of victim rather than challenge the protagonist. We often fail to acknowledge our personal power, neither questioning others' assertions nor standing up for our rights. However, a conflict which is not acknowledged does have a tendency to develop to an extent where its resolution becomes even more difficult. People are likely to avoid acknowledging a problem if they hold false assumptions such as: conflicts are always bad; keeping quiet makes the problem go away; confronting a problem creates further tension and aggression; there is little anyone can do to influence the outcome of the problem; someone will always be the loser.

Planning action. Once you have acknowledged that a conflict exists, the next step is to plan the action you will take. This clearly requires careful thought, as you are bound to have strong feelings about the other person and the reasons behind the conflict. At the one extreme, you may feel threatened or inhibited, at the other you may feel irritated or angry. The former may lead you to be less than honest about the problem, while the latter may lead you to be aggressive and blaming. The ideal would be to state exactly how you feel, calmly and rationally. You may find it helpful to write down beforehand what your thoughts and feelings are, what you intend to say and how you will say it, how you will take action and what you would like to achieve. You may also find that it is helpful to discuss this with someone whose views and opinions you trust before putting it into action.

Alerting the other party. Once you have planned the action you will take, the next step involves alerting the other party. In doing so it is important to: tell them what you think the problem is; state how you feel; state what you want; and let the other party know that you want them to behave differently.

Enlisting their co-operation. Enlisting the other party's co-operation is likely to be even more difficult than stating how you feel. There is always a danger that they will refuse to acknowledge that a conflict exists, perhaps even respond aggressively, claiming that it is your problem and not theirs.

It is important to remember that we all have established views of ourselves but these may be at odds with the views that others hold of us. There may then be a genuine difference between two people with regard to their perception of events.

Because we all have established views of ourselves, it is likely that any challenge we make to another's behaviour will be marked by a degree of defensiveness. It is important to recognize that the manner in which a challenge is presented can have a considerable influence on the response to it. A challenge will generate a negative reaction if it is stated with an element of superiority or if it appears to be manipulative rather than a genuine request for change.

If the other party refuses to acknowledge a problem, perceiving your attempts to do so as a personal challenge, it is important to weigh up whether a further attempt to engage the other person in co-operative problem-solving will be worthwhile. Repeated rebuffs can be damaging to your sense of self-worth. It is important to remember that you can only be responsible for your own thoughts, feelings and behaviour and not those of someone else.

UNDERSTANDING EACH OTHER'S POSITION

Attempting to gain a clearer understanding of each other's position is valuable for a number of reasons:

- It allows both parties involved to establish whether there is a real problem or whether they have simply misunderstood or misperceived the situation.

- Once this has been established, differing views about the situation can be aired.

- The opportunity to air views is, in itself, a means of diffusing any pent-up emotions or tension. This is necessary before rational discussion of the problem can take place.

- Seeking out the other person's perception of the situation shows that you value them as a work colleague and that you are prepared to work with them to resolve any problems which exist.

In order to fully understand each other it is necessary for each party to endeavour to make a clear and specific statement of their respective positions; listen to the other and not let emotions get in the way of hearing what is being said; and try to avoid apportioning blame.

It is often useful to ask direct questions with follow-up questions as necessary. In order to be direct without being interrogative simple questions will suffice: 'How do you see the problem?'; 'Could you clarify how you see your role?'; 'Why do you think we got into this situation?'.

Seeing the world through someone else's eyes is no easy matter. Two peoples' perceptions of the same event almost invariably differ. To see if you fully appreciate the other person's point of view, it can be useful to restate their position in your own words. Questions beginning, 'So what you are saying is . . .' or 'From your point of view you thought that . . . ' will in turn generate correction and comment, and help to indicate the extent to which mutual understanding is being achieved.

In order to state your own position, it is important to be precise and open without blaming the other party. Statements such as these might be useful: 'From my point of view it would have been better if you had told me directly'; 'I did not see that as your responsibility'; 'I would have found it helpful if, in the first instance, it could have been discussed at the appropriate committee'.

While you may not wish to involve a third party in your dispute, it is sometimes desirable to do so. We are often more adept at stating our own position than listening to another person's viewpoint. Someone not directly involved, but whom both parties trust, can facilitate communication, diffuse emotional tension and reflect upon what is being said (see Chapter 6).

DISCUSSING THE PROBLEM AND POSSIBLE SOLUTIONS

Having presented both sides of the conflict, the aim of the third phase is to try to arrive at a mutually acceptable solution to the problem. This is clearly a difficult process, particularly given that your usual way of interacting with the other party is likely to have involved the use of power-plays rather than mutual problem-solving strategies. The power struggle of an 'I win – you lose' way of operating may well be carried over into any discussion of the problem. Each participant may state their position repeatedly in an attempt to be seen in a positive light while the other party is presented in a negative light. Collaborative problem-solving is only possible if both parties have a genuine desire to resolve the conflict and have sufficient respect for each other to pursue such a course. Constructive problem-solving can be facilitated by recognizing the factors likely to promote a Win–Lose or Lose–Lose outcome. In order to work towards a Win–Win solution, parties should attempt to: identify and acknowledge common ground; acknowledge that both parties contribute in some way to the conflict; acknowledge that both parties have particular needs; focus upon real rather than peripheral concerns; be clear and precise.

RESOLVING THE PROBLEM IN A MUTUALLY ACCEPTABLE WAY

If the previous stages have been fully addressed, it should now be possible to generate solutions to the conflict. Not all such solutions will be mutually acceptable and it is important for both parties to weigh up the alternatives, making sure that they know how the other party thinks and feels about each possible solution. In doing so, it is useful to bear the following concerns in mind:

- Is the solution fair to both parties?
- Are both parties equally satisfied with the solution?

RESOLVING CONFLICTS WITH COLLEAGUES

EXERCISE 6

Think of a colleague with whom you have an acknowledged conflict and complete the following:

1. *Recognize the problem*
▶ Is the problem important enough to acknowledge?

[You might find it helpful to assess the costs and benefits of confronting the conflict (see Chapter 1). Do the benefits of confronting the conflict outweigh the costs of not doing so?]

▶ List any reasons you can think of for both confronting and not confronting the conflict.

[Which list is longer? Was it easier to think of reasons for not confronting the conflict? Are your reasons for not confronting the conflict overly pessimistic? If your answer to any or all of these questions is 'yes', you may not be acknowledging your own personal power fully.]

2. *Try to understand each other's position*
▶ Write down your own thoughts and feelings about the conflict.
▶ Try to put yourself in the other person's shoes and write down your perception of how the other person thinks and feels about the conflict and what thoughts or feelings he or she attributes to you.

[Remember that different people often perceive the same situation in very different ways, so try to explore all options, even if they do not appear to be immediately obvious to you.]

3. *Discuss the problem*
▶ How would you define the problem? Would the other person's definition of the problem differ? If so, how?
▶ How do you think the other person perceives their own contribution, if any, to the conflict?
▶ What is your perception of your own, if any, contribution to the problem?
▶ Is there a hidden agenda? What do you think it is?
▶ Is there any common ground between you? What is it?

4. *Resolve the problem*
▶ What is your preferred solution to the problem?
▶ What are the advantages and disadvantages of your solution?
▶ Is it a combative (I win – you lose) or a collaborative (I win – you win) solution?
▶ Is it fair to both parties?
▶ Would your solution create resentment?
▶ Is it the solution the other party would arrive at? If not, how would it differ?
▶ How would your solution be implemented? Would you use a third party?

- Would the solution leave any residual resentment?
- Are both parties' rights and obligations clearly stated and fully understood?

Finally, a clear contract, agreed upon by both parties, should be drawn up. This may include definitions of each person's roles and responsibilities, a delineation of the rules of conduct and perhaps specific rules for avoiding or solving future conflict. Although any contract should be open to re-negotiation, this should always involve bilateral rather than unilateral action.

Attempting to negotiate a resolution to a conflict is not always successful and conflicts frequently persist. It is important to recognize that a sincere attempt to resolve differences was made and that one can only be responsible for one's own actions. Occasionally the intervention of a third party such as a union representative or manager can help. On other occasions it may be necessary to live with the differences although this may not be possible. Under these circumstances, it may be necessary to examine other ways of extracting oneself from difficult relationships at work. This may involve using the appropriate complaints procedure, seeking a transfer to a different department or, ultimately, seeking alternative employment. These issues are discussed in Chapter 6.

Chapter Four

Difficulties in Professional Relationships

There is a wide range of contexts in which professionals come into contact with members of the general public. These include patient or client contact for doctors, nurses, social workers and psychologists; student and parent contact for teachers and lecturers; and the everyday contact that the police have with members of the public. As noted in Chapter 1, all relationships are governed by a set of informal rules – professional relationships are no exception. Indeed, professional bodies often serve to formalize specific rules of conduct as a set of guidelines or ethics. Just as the behaviour of the caregiver, educator or police officer is governed by rules, so too is the behaviour of the recipient.

Clearly, professional relationships can and do vary – length of contact and intimacy and intensity of the relationship being notable instances. A police officer may encounter a member of the general public for a few seconds or minutes and have no or limited contact with them thereafter; a doctor may see a patient for a few minutes on just one or a restricted number of occasions; a nurse may encounter the same patient a number of times a day for several days; a teacher is likely to spend a considerable amount of time each day throughout the year with the same pupils. A close bond may develop between teacher and pupil, with the relationship being similar to a parent–child relationship in certain respects. Some professional relationships, such as therapist–client, demand a high degree of disclosure on intimate topics. Unlike friendships or other intimate relationships, however, this disclosure is non-reciprocal; it is assumed that only the client will self-disclose. Despite the variations between them, all professional relationships are based on a shared understanding – a common set of assumptions about how each should behave.

CHARACTERISTICS OF PROFESSIONAL RELATIONSHIPS

Although professional relationships are in many ways similar to all other relationships, there are certain unique aspects which require consideration. There is an assumption, for example, that those vested with particular professional skills and knowledge possess authority and hence hold a certain amount of power within the relationship. The relationship rules reflect this – one person provides a diagnosis, treatment and/or information, while the other describes a problem, listens to advice or learns. While this power imbalance does exist, it is clearly open to abuse from both sides. The person in whom power is invested might, on the one hand, be too dismissive or show a lack of interest. On the other hand, they may be too friendly or intimate. A client might be too deferential or, conversely, too demanding. Ideally, interactions between professionals and patients, clients or students will involve an active partnership, with the particular professional helping the other person to help themselves. As with all relationships, however, interpersonal conflicts may well occur in professional relationships.

Although there might be clear instances of rule breaking or manipulation of power within professional relationships, such encounters are also prone to misunderstanding. Misunderstandings can arise both as a result of false beliefs or assumptions about the rules governing such relationships, and as a result of the use of professional jargon. It is not unusual for professionals to use terms familiar to their own group which are not familiar to, or which are interpreted differently by, the general public. Use of professional jargon can be a major barrier to effective communication, and could result, for example, in a client's failure to continue with therapy or co-operate in their treatment. Such clients might be viewed as difficult by the caregiver with a subsequent deterioration of the professional–client relationship.

Conflicts within professional relationships are governed by three main factors:

1. Factors inherent in the relationship, that is, the acceptance or non-acceptance of the rule structure governing such relationships.

2. Factors related to the characteristics and personalities of the people concerned and how they evaluate and treat others.

3. Factors related to the evaluation of the situation, that is, the extent to which the language used and the different assumptions of the parties concerned generate misunderstandings.

The extent of the conflict will depend upon the degree to which both parties follow the rules, share power, have common assumptions and communicate effectively. There may be 'difficult encounters' which are relatively easy to manage. These involve minimal rule breaking, a marginally unacceptable power imbalance and/or some degree of misunderstanding. At the extreme, there are 'challenging encounters' where rule breaking is rife and power is openly questioned, with each party determined not to understand the other. Indeed, such encounters may contain elements of manipulative intent and threat, and they may sometimes act as precursors to openly aggressive and occasionally violent behaviour. In dealing with challenging encounters, one aim is to prevent them from developing further. (For a discussion of violence and aggression in professional relationships see Breakwell, 1989.) At an intermediate level, there are 'manipulative encounters' where the two parties are battling for control, neither being sure where the power lies nor how the rules are being used.

RULES OF PROFESSIONAL RELATIONSHIPS

From their research, Argyle and Henderson (1985) have identified a broad set of informal rules governing teacher–pupil and doctor–patient relationships. The following lists are an extension of these rules. As with relationships in general, those involving professional contact are bi-directional so that rules also govern the behaviour of the recipient.

RULES OF BEHAVIOUR FOR PROFESSIONAL CAREGIVERS

◊ Listen carefully to patient/clients. They have often lived with their problem for a long time and can contribute valuable insight and knowledge.

◊ Explain everything carefully to the patient/client and check back on their comprehension.

◊ Offer appropriate counselling and support or recognize the need and refer elsewhere.

◊ Be open and honest as this will help to gain the patient's/client's respect which will, in turn, facilitate compliance with treatment.

◊ Respect patient's/client's wishes; it is vital to get their full co-operation and not to impose decisions on them.

◊ Treat information provided by the patient/client with the strictest confidence.

◊ Do not criticize the patient publicly or discuss them with others except, if it is appropriate, with qualified colleagues.

◊ Do not become personally involved with the patient/client or engage in sexual activity with them.

◊ Although there may be instances when revealing your own feelings or anxieties is appropriate and, indeed, can facilitate the therapeutic relationship, there are times when this is inappropriate and, in some professions, discouraged.

◊ Do not expect practical assistance from patients. Their role is to assist you in the task of assisting them.

RULES OF BEHAVIOUR FOR PATIENTS/CLIENTS

□ Ask for clarification as appropriate.

□ Follow instructions/treatment/advice or question if appropriate.

□ Provide all information necessary for the professional concerned to formulate diagnosis/treatment.

□ Be open and honest; misleading or hidden information hinders treatment.

□ Do not make 'unreasonable' demands on the professional caregiver's time.

□ Respect the professional caregiver's privacy.

RULES OF BEHAVIOUR FOR TEACHERS

● Be well informed about the subject matter you are teaching and prepare teaching sessions thoroughly.

● Criticism should be constructive and feedback timely and adequate.

● Be fair in your treatment of all pupils/students.

- Seek to answer questions but also admit ignorance when necessary.

- Be approachable and make yourself available when necessary.

- Offer emotional support as appropriate.

- Keep appropriate control and discipline.

- Respect the privacy of pupils and students.

- Do not engage in sexual activity with pupils/students.

RULES OF BEHAVIOUR FOR STUDENTS

- Put forward your views and stand up for them.

- Show initiative and ask questions as appropriate.

- Accept constructive criticism.

- Prepare work and hand it in on time.

- Co-operate with the teacher and follow directions, but do not be overly submissive.

- Respect the teacher's privacy.

- Do not engage in sexual activity with the teacher.

These rules paint a rather one-sided picture, suggesting that conflict would be minimal if the professional listens and explains in a clear and friendly way to a client who receives and acts upon instructions. This creates the impression that the 'bad' client is one who fails to adhere to instructions, treatment or advice, or who fails to give all the necessary information. This may indeed be the case in many instances. However, the client's beliefs and experiences do not always match those of the professional concerned and this may lead to conflict if the professional is unable to recognize or accept the client's position. Clients need to be seen as active participants in decision-making. Certainly, research in medical contexts suggests that patients who are actively involved in treatment programmes, who are informed of the treatment rationale and encouraged to ask questions are far more satisfied with the consultation process. The same no doubt applies to other professional relationships.

DIFFICULT PROFESSIONAL RELATIONSHIPS

DETERMINANTS OF RULE-BREAKING BEHAVIOUR

It is generally presumed that people will have shared assumptions about the informal rules governing behaviour. If certain people are not aware of these rules, or do not possess the necessary skills to effectively execute the behaviour prescribed by the rules, they may break the rules unintentionally. There are other factors, however, which prompt people to intentionally stretch or break rules. A person's behaviour always reflects their individual background, needs and personality. Some people are, by nature, less co-operative or more likely to gain satisfaction from aggressive encounters. Certain personality characteristics are associated with how difficult or satisfactory a professional relationship is likely to be. These include the extent to which the client is dependent or independent, hostile or friendly, co-operative or uncooperative, and the extent to which they reject or accept information or treatment. Any person at the extreme of these scales, that is too dependent, too friendly, too uncooperative or too accepting, may well create difficulties for the professional concerned.

It is important to bear in mind, however, the bi-directional nature of relationships and that the conflict may, in fact, be the responsibility of the professional concerned. The overly hostile, forceful or superior professional and, conversely, the over-concerned or over-friendly professional is likely to play a part in generating conflict with clients.

Background characteristics, such as education and social environment, serve to shape beliefs and expectations. Beliefs about professionals range from the unrealistically positive (the 'miracle worker' perspective) to the completely negative (the 'worse than useless' perspective). A client in awe of a professional may have unrealistically high expectations or may constantly seek help. On the other hand, a client who needs to denigrate the professional may blame him or her for everything or may even become threatening or abusive. The aim of professional relationships is to serve the best interests of the client, with the assumption that conflicts of interest will be minimal. Nevertheless, all relationships are open to manipulation, both by professionals and their clients, and this needs to be addressed.

MANIPULATION

Manipulation of one person by another implies the ability to influence people in specific ways. Indeed, all the caring professions are involved in influencing behaviour in one way or another, and could thus be regarded as manipulative. There is, in fact, a fine line between manipulating and helping. When helping, the professional's motives are likely to be open and shared with the client. Manipulation, however, is more likely to have unstated motives or some hidden purpose, while the impression is created that the manipulator is not responsible for what is happening. In view of this, manipulation is more likely to be used by those in less powerful positions against a powerful other, rather than vice versa. There are exceptions, however, such as sexual intimacies of teachers with students or doctors/therapists with patients, where manipulation merges with a misuse of power.

The following features have been isolated as factors common to cases in which a person without authority or direct power influences an apparently powerful other.

☐ In a manipulative relationship, the client's motives or needs will not be immediately clear to the professional. Thus, while the patient or student may describe physical symptoms or work-related problems, the hidden agenda relates to a desire for attention or emotional support.

☐ A manipulative client will seek to emphasize the special nature of their relationship with the professional. The patient or student may try to engineer the professional's 'attachment' by offering expressions of gratitude or praise and by making references to the professional's specialness. Typical comments include: 'You're the only one who really understands my problem' or 'Everyone says you're the best teacher'.

☐ Skilled manipulators try to exploit professionals' 'dependency' upon them. It might seem that unlike the client who appears to be entirely dependent upon the professional for therapy or educational input, the professional is not in any way dependent upon the client. However, by using praise or expressions of gratitude, it is possible for the client to trap the carer or teacher into feeling that they are, in essence, the only ones who can help. Patient and therapist or teacher and student then become mutually dependent, with the therapist or teacher providing (or trying to provide) more and more help.

□ Good manipulators are very sensitive to the motives and needs of others. The skilled manipulator will recognize if a nurse, doctor or therapist is particularly caring or if a policeman or teacher has been exceptionally helpful and will seek to exploit such characteristics. It is important to recognize that the manipulative client may have identified particular weaknesses or needs of the professional concerned and is using this knowledge for his or her own purposes. Professionals constantly need to be aware of their responsibilities in order to maintain the boundaries appropriate to professional relationships.

□ A further characteristic of manipulators is that they influence in bits and pieces. They let the professional win one step and then move them along to another position. Thus, a client may thank a doctor or therapist for curing or helping them, but will then return with a new symptom or problem. This may create anxiety or self-doubt on the part of the professional who may feel that 'perhaps something was overlooked'. However, they will subsequently be reassured by the patient or client when the next symptom or problem is dealt with. Clearly, a client who overplays this pattern of behaviour may cause irritation, perhaps resulting in their referral to another professional.

MISUSE OF POWER

One issue that has been the topic of much recent research is that of the professional who exceeds the boundaries of friendship or who engages in sexual intimacy with clients. Studies in the United States suggest that this is not an uncommon problem. One anonymous survey of graduate students indicated that 17 per cent had had sexual contact with at least one of their teachers during their training (Glaser and Thorpe, 1986). A further national survey reported that 13 per cent of therapists had sexual contact with current or recent clients (Holroyd and Brodsky, 1977). A finding from both surveys was that the majority of sexual liaisons involved men in the powerful professional role and women in the less powerful student or patient role. In a summary of prevalence studies published in the last 15 years, Pope (1988) notes that 8.3 per cent of male therapists reported engaging in therapist–client sex, compared to 1.7 per cent for women. There is no doubt a great deal of overlap between sexual intimacy in professional relationships and sexual harassment – the figures above are remarkably similar to those obtained from earlier surveys of sexual harassment from a number of university campuses. Clearly, sexual intimacies within educator and student or therapist/doctor and patient relationships contain the distinct possibility of being either covertly or overtly coercive. Such behaviour is likely to be exploitative and potentially harmful and is regarded as unethical within professional guidelines. Studies suggest that the majority of people also view sexual relationships between professionals and their clients as coercive, harmful, unethical and a major hindrance to the working relationship. The range of harmful consequences includes an inability to trust; guilt, anger and confusion; depression and increased suicide risk (Pope, 1988).

DIFFICULT CLIENTS

Patients who create problems for their doctors have been labelled 'hateful' by the psychiatrist James Groves (1978). This is clearly a rather strong term to describe those patients who kindle fear, dislike or aversion in caregivers. Nevertheless, it provides a useful framework for considering difficult professional–client relationships. He suggests that there are four types of 'hateful' or problem patients. Although these have been derived from the context of doctor–patient relationships, they apply equally to other professional relationships.

THE DEPENDENT CLINGER
In the medical context, this refers to repeat attenders who do not appear to have any clearly identifiable condition and who constantly seek attention, reassurance, explanation and affection. They are often referred to as being hypochondriacal, although this term has unfortunate negative connotations and such patients can perhaps more appropriately be viewed as being excessively anxious about their health. Although it is almost automatic to provide these patients with reassurance, research suggests that this may actually be counterproductive, serving to reduce anxiety only in the short-term with an actual increase in anxiety over the longer term. Reassurance may thus serve to reinforce the attendance of such patients at surgeries. Examples of the dependent clinger in other contexts are:

- The person who regularly contacts the police about suspected intruders or suspicious people near to their home, each instance proving to be a false alarm.

- The client who states that they will be unable to cope without another appointment with the therapist.
- The student who is unable to take a decision, even about seemingly trivial matters, without first consulting their teacher.
- The parent who is unable to manage their child without constantly seeking advice from the teacher.

Some professional relationships involving long-term therapist–client contact actually foster dependency. In such cases, the therapist needs to be sufficiently skilled to ensure that the client can cope at termination of therapy. However, at times, professionals can foster such dependence unwittingly, either because they have been manipulated to do so or because client dependency serves to fulfil their own needs.

The dependent clinger may become overbearing; in extreme cases, seeking help or advice on a daily basis or intruding into the professional's private life at home. Regaining control if the situation is allowed to reach this extreme level is no easy matter, and great tact and assertion will be necessary. It is clearly desirable to prevent the situation from escalating to this stage.

THE 'ENTITLED' DEMANDER

In the medical context, although it is quite usual to expect to receive a certain treatment or be able to ask for a second opinion, the 'entitled' demander is a patient who feels that they have an unquestioning right to such treatment and demand it in an unreasonable and aggressive manner. It could equally apply, however, in other contexts. Examples include the person who believes that:

- The social worker should resolve all their social needs.
- The police officer should find their stolen possessions immediately.
- The therapist must 'cure' their problem.
- The teacher must meet all the emotional and educational needs of each pupil.

The entitled demander may resort to threats to achieve their objective. Emotional blackmail, threats of legal action or threats of physical violence are more common than actual physical violence – although this may occur if the situation is allowed to escalate. The entitled demander may genuinely be anxious about their health, social situation or child's well-being, but they cope by directing their emotional energy at the professional rather than attempting to alter the situation. It is thus all too easy to become entangled in an unproductive debate with them. Ideally, the threatening nature of the situation needs to be diffused and the client's energy channelled towards problem-solving.

THE MANIPULATIVE HELP REJECTOR

In the medical context, this refers to the patient who believes that no treatment will actually help, so that when one symptom is cured, others develop. Other examples include:

- The client who assures the therapist that they will try to institute the suggested action while simultaneously stating they are sure it will not help.
- Parents who ask for help with a difficult child and who return within a matter of days saying the suggested advice did not work, even though they were told of the need to persevere as any change would occur after weeks or months rather than days.

In many ways, what the manipulative help rejector fears most is losing the help they are being offered. Their actions slowly draw the professional into a frustrating relationship. Again tact and assertive repetition of advice can help, although the patient or student concerned may well assign themselves to someone else whom they feel will fulfil their needs, and hence the problem passes along with them.

THE SELF-DESTRUCTIVE DENIER

In the medical context, this refers to the patient who refuses to acknowledge the existence of a problem while persisting in the very activity likely to exacerbate the problem. For example, the person with high blood pressure who persists in engaging in a range of high stress activities even when told this might endanger his or her health. Again this applies equally in other contexts. For example:

- The student whose social activities predominate over study activities even when he or she is told that this will lead to failure.

Although for some people denial can, in the short-term, be an effective way of coping with stress, self-destructive denial is a very different matter. The person concerned seems intent on defeating all attempts to help them. Such patients or students can evoke feelings of extreme frustration on the part of the professional trying to provide the help. In such instances, it is clearly important to recognize the boundaries of one's professional responsibilities.

GAMES IN PROFESSIONAL RELATIONSHIPS

The way in which professionals can become embroiled with manipulative clients has been clearly illustrated by Eric Berne in his book *Games People Play* (1964). He describes a game as a transaction or social encounter between two or more people where there is a concealed motive but a well-defined, predictable outcome. More specifically, he refers to a range of 'consulting room games' which are played in the therapeutic situation. These include games called 'I'm only trying to help you' (ITHY) played by the therapist or care worker and 'wooden leg' (WL) played by patients or clients. He distinguishes people who play ITHY from helpers who offer advice to patients such as 'I think we can do something about it'. This is offered in good faith as professional help while those who play ITHY have more complex motives, including the need for reassurance. ITHY refers to instances when a therapist colludes with the 'manipulative help rejector' by repeatedly giving advice to the patient who returns, reporting that the suggestion did not have the desired effect. The therapist who becomes embroiled in this game will try again and again, each time facing a patient who claims the treatment has failed; the process is repeated ad infinitum. In the worst case scenario, the patient may then blame the therapist if things go wrong ('Look what you made me do') resulting in the therapist's spoken or unspoken thought 'But I was only trying to help you' and bewilderment at the patient's ingratitude. Although the game ITHY is prompted by the therapist's desire to help, it is also prompted by a desire to be perceived as competent in the face of patients whom they fear make them appear incompetent.

The game 'wooden leg' is likely to be played by a patient who is also a self-destructive denier. It refers to the notion that we find excuses to explain our behaviour rather than attempt to change, seeking to blame an object, person or situation (that is, the metaphorical 'wooden leg') rather than accepting personal responsibility for our actions (that is, 'What can I do given my circumstances?'). If the professional plays along with the client, any therapeutic progress will be minimal; but those who challenge the excuse are likely to be caught in a frustrating contest of wills that is difficult to resolve. Berne suggests that the therapist should decline both options, instead helping the patient redefine what they expect of themselves. In attempting to limit game playing, it is important to recognize and address the motives of both parties.

It is important for professionals to recognize that they, like everyone else, have insecurities and needs. Certain patients may strike a raw nerve or raise delicate topics, making the professional wary or closed to the problem, or causing them to reflect on their ability to remain objective. For example, the therapist who is experiencing marital difficulties or whose close relative is severely depressed may find it difficult to deal with a client with marital problems or depression. Even the best training cannot prepare professionals for all eventualities and many training programmes fail to address such concerns. When faced with such circumstances, it is important not only to acknowledge the feeling the patient generates, but also to know when to refer a client to a colleague or when to discuss concerns with colleagues.

In addition, many professionals may not only like to be liked, they may also feel the need to be seen as persons of worth by others. This is a particularly striking feature of the game ITHY. While it is perhaps easier to see patients as 'hateful', it is important to be aware of how needs and insecurities can affect a professional's own perceptions and behaviour.

DEALING WITH DIFFICULT PROFESSIONAL RELATIONSHIPS

Three aspects of dealing with difficult clients are described here: the need to recognize professional boundaries and responsibilities; the need to set limits and say 'no'; and the ability to diffuse a potentially threatening situation.

PROFESSIONAL BOUNDARIES AND RESPONSIBILITIES

Both informal rules of conduct and professional guidelines delineate the responsibilities associated with a particular job. As a professional, it is vital to acknowledge and accept these responsibilities in order to reduce the potential for conflict. A professional's responsibilities include: adhering to ethical and other professional constraints; not misusing one's position for personal gain;

acknowledging the boundaries and limits of professional responsibilities by accepting that you cannot be successful with every client and by not allowing professional relationships to intrude into your private life; and acknowledging errors rather than blaming others. One should seek to rectify errors, learn from mistakes and try not to repeat them.

SETTING LIMITS AND SAYING 'NO'

What are your own needs? While some clients are undoubtedly more dependent or demanding than others, our own actions can serve to encourage dependency and may even serve to fulfil our own needs rather than those of the client. Any professional would appreciate being thanked for their advice and help. However, too great a need to be appreciated can actively encourage certain clients to seek more and more advice and help. Initially this is rewarding, it is only when it becomes intrusive and overbearing that problems may arise.

Recognize your pattern of thinking. As noted in previous chapters, we often have unrealistic expectations of ourselves which relate to our needs but which also act as barriers to action. Carers, in particular, might be at risk of thinking that, 'I must always be nice' or 'I must always be liked'. Always saying 'yes' might make us feel nicer or more liked in the short-term, but as noted, only serves to encourage clinging and dependence. Saying 'no' to a dependent or demanding client may temporarily cast us in the guise of the 'bad guy' but it is in the client's interests to do so and may actually lead to the client valuing or respecting us more in the long-term.

Recognizing your feelings. Situations in which you have to cope with someone else's difficult behaviour, especially if this means altering your own typical pattern of reacting or thinking, can be anxiety-provoking. Identifying your aims, planning your action and sticking to your aims while remaining calm and rational are helpful strategies in dealing with difficult situations.

What is your contribution to the situation? It is almost always easier to see someone else as being responsible for difficult situations. One is more likely to see a client as being demanding or dependent than to recognize that our own reactions might encourage or facilitate such behaviour. Consequently, changing the situation may entail altering one's own position rather than directly seeking to change the client's.

What are the advantages and disadvantages of being assertive? Given the different types of difficult clients, there are clearly occasions when assertiveness might be counterproductive. A hostile client might become even more threatening and destructive if challenged, a dependent client might simply seek alternative care where their established pattern of behaviour will continue. But assertively informing an overly dependent person that their behaviour is unacceptable, if handled tactfully, should result in a modification of their behaviour.

DIFFUSING PHYSICALLY THREATENING SITUATIONS

A teacher confronted by an angry parent or pupil, a police officer approaching a group of hostile youths or a doctor dealing with a distraught and angry patient all, no doubt, hope that the situation does not escalate to one of open aggression or violence. There are a number of steps professionals can take to decrease the chances of such an outcome:

▶ Remain calm, at least outwardly, at all times. Take a deep breath, breathe evenly and think positively. Keep telling yourself, 'I can handle this', 'I can remain calm'.

▶ As a corollary to the above, avoid revealing your feelings at all times. Think carefully about what you say and control your facial expressions, gestures and posture. The following guidelines will help in this regard:
  − Retain eye contact: do not be evasive or try to dominate the other person by staring at them.
  − Maintain an upright posture so that your head is neither tucked down nor too much 'in the air'.
  − Keep your hand movements open and even, avoiding fidgeting or clenched fists.
  − Speak at a steady even pace, do not hesitate or make clipped statements.
  − Speak in a steady and firm tone, speak neither too quietly nor too sharply.

▶ Try to achieve a balance between being too assertive and too weak. It is important to take into consideration how forceful to be or how much 'muscle' to exhibit. Any sign of anger on your part may well lead to further aggression from the aggressor. Conversely, fear or hesitation on your part may well be

ANALYSING DIFFICULT PROFESSIONAL RELATIONSHIPS

EXERCISE 7

❏ *Ben is an unemployed father of three children who has a reputation for drinking and aggression. His children are badly cared for and frequently covered in bruises. He collects them from school but is always late, unkempt and surly. On one occasion, his eldest daughter cut herself at school, and although the injury was only minor, she went to hospital as a precaution. Unfortunately, the school was unable to contact and inform the parents of their daughter's injury prior to the end of the school day. When the class teacher attempted to explain his daughter's injury to him, the father shouted at her, threatening her and telling her it was her responsibility to make sure his child was safe at school.*

❏ *Ray is middle-aged, unemployed and single. He regularly visits his GP with various aches and pains. He has been referred to the general hospital for tests on a number of occasions but results are always negative. He has frequently called his GP at unsocial hours, usually prefacing his call with comments such as, 'You're always so understanding'. He insists that there is something physically wrong with him and has told his doctor. 'If anyone can find the problem I know you can'.*

1. Think about both situations and describe their key features. In particular think about the following questions.

▶ What informal rules, if any, do you think have been broken?
▶ Which characteristics of the parent or patient do you think are particularly difficult? Do they fit any of the categories of difficult clients described above?
▶ What do you think are the parent's or patient's needs? In what way is either being manipulative?
▶ What part, if any, do you think the teacher or doctor has to play in the situation?

2. How should the teacher deal with the aggressive father?

3. How should the doctor deal with the demanding patient?

interpreted as signs of weakness resulting in the aggressor 'coming in for the kill'. If you are likely to encounter the parent or patient on subsequent occasions, it is particularly important that they are not left feeling resentful as a result of being defeated, or believing that hostility can be used to achieve their goal.

▶ Let the other person have their say, but try to direct them towards issues or concerns rather than allowing them to mount a personal attack. Ask the hostile parent or patient to tell you exactly what the problem is so that you will be able to help them.

▶ Try to engineer the situation so that you can leave, even temporarily, so that someone else can be contacted. Make an excuse in the guise of helping. For example, you might state that you need to collect their child's or the patient's records from another room in order to deal with their complaint or problem. The aim is to give yourself an opportunity to return with colleagues if necessary.

While it is undoubtedly possible to delineate categories of difficult clients, it is important to recognize that, as with all difficult relationships, both parties and their manner of interaction contribute to problems. As a professional, it is important to be aware of one's own insecurities and needs and to recognize when these are likely to impede the professional–client relationship. It is also important to be alert to situations where one is drawn into giving too much help or persisting with help when it is inappropriate. Unfortunately, not all professional training programmes address such issues. Many professionals gain valuable support from colleagues and many departments provide forums for case discussion or peer support. General discussion of cases can help to highlight the issues raised in this chapter pertaining to needs, professional boundaries and limits.

Chapter Five

Harassment at Work

As noted in previous chapters, interpersonal conflicts can range from minor disagreement to overt hostility. The various factors influencing whether relationships will be harmonious or in conflict include group and relationship issues, personality differences and the meaning attributed to certain behaviours. Reference has also been made to the fact that interpersonal conflicts at work are sometimes due to the fixed perceptions and beliefs that some people hold about others; for example, that older people are more inflexible or unable to adapt to new ideas. At the extreme, however, certain people are selected for attack purely because of their physical characteristics or emotional make-up. Discriminatory treatment of the person because of his or her membership of a particular group, usually sexual or racial, can take many forms. At one level this might involve denial of a job or promotion. This is reflected in the fact that women and members of racial minority groups receive lower than average salaries in comparison to the population as a whole, and occupy less top grade positions at work in comparison to white male employees with similar qualifications and experience. One study, for example, found that black applicants for a range of jobs, including skilled, manual and secretarial work, were much less likely to be called to interview than white applicants (Brown and Gay, 1985).

At another level, the systematic oppression and exclusion of someone singled out on grounds of race or gender can take the form of verbal abuse or physical attack. Their authority and credibility are repeatedly questioned and they are effectively rejected as equals or superiors. Such actions clearly constitute overt harassment. Sexual and racial harassment in particular, while not necessarily on the increase, have been increasingly recognized as a a major source of conflict and threat at work. Other groups singled out include lesbians and gay men and, recently, employees have refused to work alongside colleagues who have, or whom they suspect of having, AIDS. Inevitably, prejudice and ignorance serve to fuel such attacks and determine the nature and extent of such hostility.

All instances of harassment at work are extreme examples of behaviour which transgress relationship rules. Rules of support, rules relating to third parties and task-related rules are likely to be ignored or broken. Practical help on work-related tasks will be withheld and, indeed, attempts may be made to impede or hinder such activities; the victim is likely to be criticized in public and sexist or racist comments are likely to be made either in their presence or behind their backs. Transgressing the rules relating to intimacy is inherent in sexual harassment.

TWO CASE STUDIES

☐ *Jane is a 30-year-old research worker who shared an office with Peter, a male colleague of similar age and status. At first they seemed to get on well, regularly discussing their work and taking lunch together. The situation changed after Peter suggested they should meet in the evening for a meal. Jane has a regular boyfriend and did not wish to change her relationship with Peter. She politely declined his offer, explaining the situation to him. Following this, Peter continually pestered Jane for a date and would frequently touch her arms or legs or stand very close to her. Initial polite requests for him to stop went unheeded and, indeed, the unwanted attention increased. Jane found herself becoming more anxious and irritable than usual. She deliberately began dressing down at work, not using make-up and wearing trousers rather than skirts. She also tried to avoid Peter where possible. Eventually the situation led to Jane openly confronting Peter about his behaviour. Peter expressed surprise that his 'friendly' behaviour could be construed as unpleasant and their relationship deteriorated further until Jane resigned from her post.*

☐ *Raj is a nurse of Asian origin. He relates well to the majority of his colleagues with the exception of Paul, a white male nurse of similar status who regularly makes racist jokes or comments at Raj's expense. This usually happens in the presence of other colleagues, several of whom have, in the past, told Paul that his comments are not funny and that he should stop. Raj initially tried to laugh off the comments and play along with the jokes; recently he has also asked Paul to stop. On this occasion, Paul's only comment was, 'Can't you take a joke?'. Raj is becoming increasingly angry and is feeling dissatisfied with his job, which he used to enjoy. He has thought of making a formal complaint to his superior but is afraid that this will only serve to make the situation worse; possibly turning other colleagues, with whom he currently gets on well, against him. He is not sure what he should do next.*

THE NATURE OF HARASSMENT

- Harassment does not necessarily involve overt physical aggression or threats. It can consist of repeated niggles, the impact of which builds up over time, resulting in a steady escalation of interpersonal conflict.

- In some cases the perpetrator and the victim attribute different meanings to the behaviour. Even though Jane made it clear that Peter's attention was unwanted, Peter perceived his behaviour as an expression of attraction and interest. Peter may not even have acknowledged to himself that his intent was to assert himself over Jane. Although the same might be said of other forms of harassment, the intent to offend, as in Paul's case above, is usually more evident. Even so, Paul may well have perceived his behaviour as acceptable and even humorous, especially given his comment when confronted by Raj. Unfortunately, prejudice sometimes clouds a person's judgement.

- Harassment has a major psychological, emotional and work-related impact on the victim. The anxiety and irritability experienced by Jane and the anger experienced by Raj are common reactions to harassment. Raj's increasing dissatisfaction with his job and the fact that Jane actually left her job, illustrate the organizational as well as the personal costs of harassment.

- Although there are clear steps that the victim can take, harassment is not easy to deal with. Ignoring or joking about the unwanted behaviour is unlikely to make the perpetrator refrain from their actions, and telling the person to stop does not necessarily work. Victims of harassment may be seen as troublemakers by colleagues if they institute a formal complaint. However, taking action is important for the victim's self-esteem and can serve to curtail the harassment.

Although there are obvious differences between racial, sexual and other forms of discrimination and harassment, there are also commonalities between them. Where possible in this chapter, reference will be made to harassment in general, although harassment of specific groups will be referred to as appropriate. As sexual harassment has formed the focus of much recent research, illustrative facts and issues have been drawn from this area in particular.

EXPLANATIONS FOR DISCRIMINATION AND HARASSMENT

Three broad explanations have been advanced with regard to sexual harassment. These focus on biological factors, learning experiences and assumed power differences within society. Other factors include the prevailing social climate and the perpetrator's particular personality characteristics.

□ *Biological explanations.* The most simplistic explanation contends that sexual harassment results from biological forces or physical attraction. The argument is that men are more likely to engage in sexual harassment because they are inherently more aggressive and have stronger sex drives than women. Although it is very difficult to say whether male/female differences in behaviour are due to inherent biological characteristics or whether they have been acquired through the process of socialization, the available evidence tends to refute any biological explanation for such differences.

□ *Learning experiences.* A second explanation for sexual harassment centres on the notion that, during our upbringing, we learn that different behaviours are acceptable for men and for women. As mentioned in previous chapters, this encourages men to be forceful and dominant and women to be submissive and passive. Sexual harassment is thus an extreme form of learned behaviour. As with the biological explanation, this can provide an excuse for unacceptable behaviour – 'I couldn't help myself' – when, in fact, such behaviours are usually used with deliberate intent.

□ *Power differences.* A third explanation views sexual harassment as the intentional use of behaviour by one group to suppress another. Thus, as mentioned in Chapter 2, men, who are traditionally in positions of greater power or status within society, use sexual harassment as a means of maintaining their dominance over women, both in the workplace and in society in general. Such behaviour is no doubt fuelled by socialization processes. As women are still more likely to be employed in lower status jobs at work, men are placed in positions where they can use their power to demand sexual favours from women.

The view that sexual harassment is behaviour intended to preserve one group's position of greater status and power, applies equally to explanations of harassment of other groups within society. All forms of discrimination can be explained, in part, by showing how one group can advance its own interests by excluding or subordinating another. This behaviour is fuelled by detrimental ethnic, gender or sexual stereotypes which label people in particular ways simply on the basis of group membership.

☐ *Prevailing social climate.* Although the structure of society has much to do with determining discrimination and harassment, the prevailing social climate at work may further influence certain people to harass others. If someone feels that their goals have been frustrated, it may be easier to direct hostility towards an innocent party from a minority group, rather than at an overtly powerful person, agency or organization. Such scape-goating is most likely to occur when a dominant group feels that competition is increasing and/or their status is being threatened, for example, during times of high unemployment or when there are restricted promotion prospects. Because scapegoating does not address the reason for the initial frustration, it does not resolve the situation and may actually generate further hostility.

☐ *Inherent personality characteristics.* Individuals who have particu-lar personality traits are more likely to discriminate against and harass others. One such trait is 'intolerance of ambiguity' – the degree to which a person is disturbed or confused by those who do or do not fit into his or her view of people and society. Lesbians and gay men may be a prime target for discrimination by such people. This may explain why many lesbians and gay men attempt to fit in by assuming a heterosexual front. Such concealment is rooted in fear of ostracism, taunts, violence and even job loss.

WHAT BEHAVIOUR CONSTITUTES HARASSMENT?

Any behaviour inflicted on a person which causes physical or emotional discomfort can be seen as harassment. To harass literally means to trouble, torment or confuse by persistent attack, questions and so on.

SEXUAL HARASSMENT

Sexual harassment is defined as any unwanted sexual attention a person (most usually a woman) experiences at work. This can include expressions and gestures such as leering, contact involving pinching or patting, verbal comments and subtle pressure for sexual activity, as well as sexual assault and rape. In response to survey questions, it appears that three-quarters of those who report sexual harassment have experienced unwanted sexual contact such as touching, pinching or cornering; sexual comments, jokes or questioning; or unwanted sexual looks or gestures (Gutek, 1985).

Surveys also suggest that the problem is a considerable one. A 1980 study conducted in the United States, found that almost half of over 10 000 women surveyed had experienced some form of unwanted and uninvited sexual attention; males who had experienced sexual harassment constituted only 15 per cent of all males sampled (US Merit Systems Protection Board, 1981). An update of this survey in 1988 found almost exactly the same percentages. Similar figures have been obtained from surveys in Europe and the United Kingdom (Stockdale, 1991). The problem seems to cut across institutions and work settings, with comparable figures obtained for women in educational establishments and health care settings, and for female secretarial staff and women managers. Surveys also suggest that in approximately two-thirds of cases the harasser is a male colleague or peer, and in one-third of cases a male superior. In particular, victims tend to be young women who are reliant on their jobs (Terpstra and Baker, 1991).

Although extreme behaviour, such as sexual assault or physical contact of a sexual nature, may be readily identified as sexual harassment, individuals interpret many sexually related actions differently. A behaviour which is perceived as mildly irritating or offensive to one person, may be perceived as sufficiently serious by someone else to warrant either reporting the incident to a superior or instigating formal complaints procedures. Surveys suggest that less than one-third of women identify sexual comments, looks or gestures which are meant to be complimentary, as sexual harassment – although they might consider the behaviour to be offensive. There is also some evidence that men and women differ in their perception of what constitutes sexual harassment. Women are twice as likely as men to identify sexual touching as harassment, and are more likely than men to identify 'complimentary' comments or suggestive remarks as harassment (Gutek, 1985).

RACIAL HARASSMENT

Racial harassment can be described as any hostile or offensive act or expression by a person of one racial or ethnic group against another; or incitement to commit such an act. The lack of any systematic survey of such events within the workplace is perhaps surprising. In comparison to sexual harassment, actions constituting racial harassment are more readily identified and less subject to differing perceptions on the part of the perpetrator and the victim. Nevertheless, the perpetrator may perceive their jokes or taunts as 'just good fun', although the behaviour is clearly offensive to the victim. A number of cases have been reported in the media of people from racial and other minority groups who have felt compelled to quit their jobs as a result of persistent taunts from colleagues, who have then expressed surprise at the victim's action. Such jokes and taunts chip away at self-esteem and may lead to feelings of helplessness, depression or anger. Other behaviours are clearly designed to offend or drive the person from work. These typically include explicit derogatory name-calling, verbal abuse, insults, ridicule, physical threats or actual assaults. Individuals can be excluded from informal groups and people can refuse to work with them.

SEXUAL ORIENTATION

Other groups are harassed in similar ways. Increasing attention has been paid to the harassment of workers because of sexual orientation. There is little documented evidence of the incidence of such harassment, although a recent United States survey of lesbian and gay students (D'Augelli, 1989) reported that three-quarters had experienced verbal abuse, one-quarter had been threatened with violence and almost one-fifth had had property damaged. The majority had made specific life changes to avoid harassment.

COSTS OF HARASSMENT

Harassment in all its forms is associated with severe personal and organizational costs. Personal costs may include a more negative attitude to work, emotional and interpersonal difficulties and physical illness. This may result in the person taking time off work or even quitting their job.

Emotional reaction. At the most basic level, the victim is likely to feel angry or helpless. Victims of sexual and racial harassment report tension, anxiety, fear, helplessness, uncontrollable anger, depression and feelings of guilt or self-blame (Loy and Stewart, 1984).

Interpersonal difficulties. Reports of divorce and marital and sexual problems are not uncommon for victims of sexual harassment. Work relationships, in general, may also be affected both because the victim may feel that colleagues are being unsupportive and also because an emotionally distressed person may be perceived by colleagues as 'not fun to be with'.

Physical illness. The more persistent the harassment, the more likely it is to be accompanied by complaints of stress-related physical illnesses, such as stomach complaints, skin disorders, headaches and loss of sleep. In one report, as many as two in ten victims felt that their physical health had suffered as a direct result of harassment (Crull, 1982).

Work-related attitudes. Harassment will almost inevitably result in a negative attitude towards work, decreased motivation and commitment. Surveys suggest that three-quarters of female victims of sexual harassment feel that their effectiveness at work suffers (Crull, 1982) and one-third feel that they become more negative in their attitudes towards their jobs (Gutek, 1985). Indeed, the victim may begin to dread work, take time off or leave their job; surveys of sexual harassment suggest as many as one-quarter of women who complain of sexual harassment leave their jobs as a direct result (Terpstra and Cook, 1985). Clearly, as well as the personal cost to the victim, there is an immense financial cost to the organization concerned which has to re-appoint and train new personnel.

DEALING WITH HARASSMENT

Harassment can be dealt with at the legislative, organizational or individual level. At the legislative level, for example, some states in the United States have recently passed bills making it unlawful employment practice to fail to take reasonable steps to prevent sexual harassment from occurring. At the organizational level, steps can be taken to increase awareness amongst employees and to specifically screen new employees for past history of harassment behaviours. It should also be the responsibility of an employer to develop specific policies relating to harassment so that channels for complaints and investigation procedures are clearly delineated. For present purposes, however, the most important issue relates to the actions an individual can take which might serve to stop the occurrence of unwanted sexual attention or other forms of harassment. The most frequently used actions tend to be:

- ignoring the behaviour by doing nothing or avoiding the perpetrator;
- reacting against the behaviour or asking the person to stop;
- making a joke of the behaviour or going along with it;
- threatening to tell others or actually reporting the behaviour to a supervisor or other official;
- taking legal action;
- quitting the job or seeking a transfer.

The action taken will depend upon a range of factors including:
- the actual and perceived severity of the harassment;
- the persistence of the harasser;
- the harasser's actual or likely response to requests to desist;
- the existence of formal workplace procedures for dealing with harassment;
- the victim's knowledge about procedures for dealing with harassment;
- the perceived attitude of management to harassment;
- the perception of management's ability to deal with harassment;
- the victim's own ability to work in the same environment should the harassment stop.

AVOIDANCE OF THE PROBLEM

Ignoring the behaviour or avoiding the person are the most commonly reported reactions to sexual harassment, particularly for less severe forms. For example, women are most likely to ignore wolf whistles and to avoid men who engage in offensive sexual jokes. However, when women are asked to report what action on their part is most likely to improve matters, asking or telling the person to stop, threatening to tell or telling others, or reporting the behaviour to a supervisor or official are seen as most likely to help. Ignoring the behaviour or doing nothing is seen as the least effective reaction. Ignoring the behaviour or avoidance are no doubt prompted by an initial reaction of disbelief and doubt, even about the most blatant acts of sexual harassment. A feeling that 'this cannot be happening to me' can result in denial – it is not unusual for a victim of sexual harassment to refuse to acknowledge that harassment has occurred or to deny the seriousness of the problem. Ignoring harassment may actually serve to increase it – the offender may interpret silence as agreement with, or even encouragement for, his behaviour. In one survey, when sexual harassment was ignored, it gradually increased in three-quarters of cases (US Merit Systems Protection Board, 1988).

Those who do acknowledge the seriousness of the harassment, may try to cope through avoidance. Avoidance of both formal and informal contact is not an unusual reaction to all kinds of harassment. As the example at the beginning of this chapter illustrates, avoidance in cases of sexual harassment can take the form of 'dressing down' – trying to appear as unattractive as possible in order to avoid being noticed. Although this may serve the desired purpose, it can also serve as an expression of self-doubt, inferiority or victimization. Attempting to ignore any form of harassment or avoiding the perpetrator may serve the victim's personal interests in the short-term, but in the longer term it is likely that the behaviour will recur or increase.

REACTING AGAINST

Individuals may react against harassment physically and/or verbally. In instances of sexual harassment, a straying hand can be effectively dealt with by a quick slap or by a comment, audible to others, which ridicules the action. Other advances may provoke physical resistance or screaming.

Verbal confrontation can either have negative or positive effects. When abuse is met with abuse or threat with threat, the conflictual situation can easily escalate. Aggressive statements such as, 'Do that again and you won't know what's hit you' are more likely to elicit defensive resistance than to encourage the protagonist to stop. More positive verbal confrontation involves asking or telling the person to stop, explaining to them why their behaviour is unwelcome. Comments such as, 'I don't like the way you keep touching me, it really isn't appropriate; we would be able to work together more effectively if you stopped' or 'I find the racist jokes you tell rather offensive; I would be grateful if you could stop' are likely to be more effective. Any such statement should explain how you feel, why you feel the way you do and request that the negative behaviour stops. Even if such requests do not have the desired result, they can nevertheless be personally rewarding. Standing up for yourself allows you to direct your anger at the appropriate target and to maintain your self-esteem.

MAKING A JOKE OF, OR PLAYING ALONG WITH, THE BEHAVIOUR

This is a potentially risky strategy to adopt and certainly is only appropriate in relation to less extreme instances of harassment. At one level, making a joke of sexist or racist comments may create a 'good' image – a reaction from others that this person takes things in his or her stride and is really 'one of us'. At another level, however, it may simply serve to encourage further harassment, particularly if the perpetrator is determined to come out on top. As any joke in this context involves colluding with the perpetrator, it is likely to be at the victim's expense and hence potentially damaging to their self-esteem. Certainly, in relation to sexual harassment, surveys suggest that less than two-fifths of those who made a joke of the behaviour and less than one-fifth of those who went along with it felt that they actually made things better by their action (US Merit Systems Protection Board, 1988).

ORGANIZATIONAL LEVEL: REPORTING THE BEHAVIOUR

Despite the high rates of sexual harassment of women, few complaints are either reported to management or pursued through official grievance procedures. Surveys of educational and social work settings suggest that about ten per cent of those who feel they have been victims of sexual harassment actually report the problem to someone in authority and only two to three per cent of victims use formal complaints channels. It is only when the harassment involves direct physical assault, promises of promotion in return for sex, or threat of job loss if sexual favours are refused that the majority of victims will follow either official internal grievance procedures or register an official complaint with an outside agency. The limited available evidence suggests that victims of racial and other forms of harassment also seldom report incidents. The failure to report harassment, unless it is extreme, is due to three main factors: many victims feel that the complaint will not be taken seriously, that no action will be taken on their behalf and that the complaining will only make the situation worse for everyone.

WILL THE COMPLAINT BE TAKEN SERIOUSLY?

A number of surveys report that as many as one-quarter of women do not feel that complaints of sexual harassment are treated either seriously or sympathetically, and many feel that they will actually be blamed for the incident if they make a formal complaint. There is also some evidence that people in senior positions do not take certain cases of sexual harassment seriously. For example, jokes with sexual connotations, pin-up calendars, suggestive remarks or leering are often not viewed as constituting sexual harassment by senior management – although they are viewed as such by female employees. There is also evidence that complaints of racial harassment are often not treated seriously.

DO ORGANIZATIONS TAKE ACTION?

Unfortunately, there is some evidence to support the fear people have that no action will be taken if they complain of harassment. In a survey of over one hundred large organizations in the United Kingdom (Davidson and Earnshaw, 1990), more than half reported that no action would be taken against someone found guilty of sexual harassment. When action is taken, it is likely to be an official or unofficial warning to the harasser. Indeed, a complaint of sexual harassment is more likely to result in the victim rather than the harasser being relocated. Such relocation may well affect promotion as any new environment will require readjustment and/or the learning of new skills. In such instances, the victim suffers twice; once as a direct result of harassment and subsequently as a result of relocation.

WILL AN OFFICIAL COMPLAINT MAKE THE SITUATION WORSE?
The failure of victims of harassment to register formal complaints is no doubt due, in some part, to the fear that there will be possible negative consequences of doing so. Indeed, in one survey, one-third of those who registered a formal complaint of sexual harassment felt that it made things worse, while ten per cent were actually fired or laid off (US Merit Systems Protection Board, 1981). Other negative work-related outcomes subsequent to complaints of sexual harassment include transfers, demotions, denied promotions, poor work evaluations and poor references. There is also the possibility that the victim may be expected to continue working with the harasser both while the complaint is being investigated and subsequent to the institution of any action, such as a warning to the harasser.

In deciding whether to report harassment, it is clearly important to weigh up the issues involved.

- The more serious the incident and/or the more persistent the harasser, the more advisable it is to report the incident.

- It is important to find out about your organization's procedures and policies for dealing with harassment and what actions or recommendations are made by your union. Does your organization have a procedure for dealing with harassment? The personnel department may have information on how to proceed. What is your organization's past record for dealing with cases of harassment? A number of trade unions in the UK (for example, the National Association of Local Government Officers, National Union of Teachers and Association of University Teachers) issue guidelines or leaflets outlining actions which can be taken by those suffering from harassment. More and more unions are taking up the issues of both sexual and racial harassment. What does your union recommend?

- Once you have reported the incident(s), will you be able to continue working in the same environment? Should you request an immediate transfer for yourself or the other person involved? If the outcome of your complaint is simply an official or unofficial warning for the harasser, would you be able to continue working with them?

THE LEGAL LEVEL

As a last resort, the victim may decide to take legal action against the harasser. This is clearly a major step to take and will require careful consideration. It is also worth bearing in mind that no law specifically prohibits harassment at work, and that if action is taken, it is dealt with under alternative, existing legislation.

THE LAW AND SEXUAL HARASSMENT

Although no law specifically prohibits sexual harassment, the *Sex Discrimination Act* (1975) in the UK, and the *Title VII Civil Rights Act* (1964) in the US can, for practical purposes, be interpreted as doing so. In the United States, sexual harassment is considered to be sex discrimination if the victim can prove that she has suffered either economic or psychological damage as a result of the behaviour. In the United Kingdom, the *Sex Discrimination Act* defines sex discrimination as less favourable treatment of a woman than a man on the grounds of sex, and makes it unlawful for an employer to discriminate against a woman by dismissing her or subjecting her to any other detriment. Previous existing legislation recognized that both employer and employee should be held responsible for anything done by a person in the course of his or her employment. However, it is a legitimate defence for the employer to prove that they took such steps as were reasonably practicable to prevent the employee from doing the act which was complained of. It is thus a matter for the courts to decide:

- whether a behaviour or verbal comment constitutes a detriment;
- whether the perpetrator of the harassment was acting in the course of his employment;
- whether the employer had taken 'such steps as were reasonably practicable' to prevent the discriminatory treatment from occurring.

Within the European Community, there is a proposal to draw up a Directive on sexual harassment. However, at present, the European Parliament has only instructed the European Commission to draw up a code of practice on the issue (Bannister, 1991).

THE LAW AND RACIAL HARASSMENT

In the UK, the *Race Relations Act* (1976) contains provisions relating to discrimination on the grounds of race, which are equivalent to those relating to sex in the *Sex Discrimination Act*. Proceedings can be brought to an Industrial Tribunal for discrimination in recruitment and promotion, as well as for matters concerning unfair dismissal, the treatment of employees and poor working conditions. Assistance can also be provided by the Commission for Racial Equality – the body established in the UK with major responsibility for implementing the *Race Relations Act*. The court would need to consider the same issues that apply in cases of sexual harassment (see page 93) before passing judgement.

WHETHER OR NOT TO TAKE LEGAL ACTION

In the UK, Industrial Tribunals are set up to deal with legal cases involving discrimination in employment, training and related fields in order to avoid the more formal and intimidating Civil Courts. It is important to bear in mind that, in the UK, there is a three-month time limit for taking legal action on any incident. In terms of procedure, the Applicant (that is, the person making the complaint) is always heard first, with an opportunity for their representative (that is, union official, appropriate organizational or legal representative) to set out the facts. Questions can then be asked by the Respondent (that is, the person against whom the complaint is made) who may also call their evidence. The Applicant can then question the Respondent.

In considering whether or not to take legal action, it is important to weigh up the pros and cons. Several issues need to be considered:

- *Litigation is complex.* In order to understand the legal issues involved, it will be necessary to obtain advice from a suitably qualified person.

- *It takes time.* What happens while litigation proceeds? Should the person be expected to remain working with the harasser?

- *It may be expensive.* Will the costs be met by the Applicant's union or another official body?

- *Is there a written record?* A written record of all incidents can be particularly important as it can be used in evidence if the case rests on the word of one person (the victim) against another (the harasser).

- *Is there a record of any correspondence?* Again, correspondence between victim and harasser can be particularly important if there are no witnesses to the harassment.

KEEPING A RECORD OF EVENTS

It is clearly important to have kept a careful record of events if you are going to register a formal complaint within your organization or, particularly, if you are considering legal action. Furthermore, Rowe (1981) has pointed out that with regard to sexual harassment, recording events can help you to deal with your own feelings, while a written letter to the perpetrator may actually stop the harassment from recurring.

1. Keep a detailed diary of each event under the following headings:
- where the incident occurred;
- the date and time;
- the exact behaviour which occurred;
- what the perpetrator said;
- what you said and did;
- any feelings associated with the event;
- details of anyone who may have witnessed the event and their reactions.

Such a record can be useful should you pursue legal action. Similar use can be made of documentary evidence from your doctor concerning psychological or physical effects of harassment.

2. Write a letter to the perpetrator. A written request can be seen to offer a challenge and often works when verbal requests to stop have failed. Rowe suggests writing the letter in three parts;

- The first part should detail all the instances of harassment as perceived by you. All the relevant facts and dates detailed in your diary should be included even if this makes the letter rather long.

- The second part should detail your feelings; express your opinion of how the event affected you ('What you said both surprised and depressed me', 'I feel extremely angry about what happened'); and detail any costs (this can include time off work or career changes).

- The final part of the letter should detail what you would like to happen next. This may well be a request for the harassment to stop ('I would like our relationship be conducted on a professional basis').

The writer of the letter should retain a copy and should make sure that it is received by the perpetrator, perhaps delivering it personally with a witness present. Such a letter can be used if either legal proceedings or an appeal to higher management proves to be necessary.

- *Is there anyone who can provide emotional support during litigation?* Given that taking legal action can be a daunting experience, emotional support is invaluable. It may also be useful to get together with others with whom one can share experiences. In the case of sexual harassment, this may be women's groups or organizations dealing specifically with women at work.

- *What are the likely outcomes?* The case may not be found in the Applicant's favour; even if it is, the most likely outcome will be an award of aggravated damages. In the past in the UK, such awards have not been high (usually less than £3,000 – often substantially less), although this may well increase (nearly £8,000 was awarded in a recent case involving sexual harassment). Industrial Tribunals can also make declarations as to the rights of the parties involved, although this is unlikely to greatly assist the victim of harassment; or they can make recommendations as to the future conduct of the parties concerned. This will also not necessarily benefit the complainant, although a recommendation can be made that the perpetrator be moved to duties away from the victim if they are still working together at the time of the hearing.

The negative outcomes of harassment are both serious and extensive. Although more organizations are recognizing the degree of the problem and the costs it imposes, both to the individual and the organization, there is still very little organizational support for such victims. It is very much up to the individual to fight back, although it is difficult to do so constructively. Our first actions are more likely to be to ignore the behaviour, make a joke of it or avoid the perpetrator. Not only are these actions ineffective, they are also likely to damage our feelings of self-worth. It is important to let the perpetrator know that you find their behaviour unacceptable and that you want it to change. Even if the desired effect of stopping their behaviour is not achieved, direct action helps to focus anger appropriately and to maintain our feelings of self-worth.

Chapter Six

When Conflicts Persist

In the first chapter, the importance of weighing up the costs and benefits of ignoring or confronting a conflict was considered. But what options are available if initial attempts to ignore the conflict are unsuccessful, or if attempts to confront it have failed? Although there are no available figures, it is likely that there is a high incidence of interpersonal conflict at work. Judging from the studies on sexual harassment, it is likely that many of these conflicts are simply ignored. In these studies, one-third to one-half of the respondents attempted either to avoid the person or to ignore the behaviour or do nothing. The more severe the harassment, the more frequently the victim sought a transfer, left their job or reported the incident, either to a supervisor or to an external agency.

Ignoring an interpersonal conflict is likely to be an appropriate action only if the conflict is truly trivial; perhaps a conflict with someone with whom we have had minimal past contact and with whom we are unlikely to work again. Similarly, a conflict which was not overly emotional or one in which issues were particularly clear cut, can be overlooked. As noted previously, however, perceptions of the situation are likely to differ between the parties involved; what is trivial to one person may not be trivial to another. One person may feel the conflict can be ignored while, for the other party, resentment grows until the conflict resurfaces, often triggered by another seemingly trivial event. If ignoring a conflict leaves any residual feelings such as anger, tension, anxiety or self-blame, then it is unlikely to be forgotten.

In addition, ignoring a conflict may actually serve to perpetuate it. If on one occasion a boss, colleague or client gets away with intrusive or abusive behaviour, what is to prevent them from trying again? A trivial event at one point in time may not be trivial if it recurs. The relative costs and benefits of ignoring a conflict are likely to change over time and it may be necessary to re-appraise your options. A conflict may persist simply because it was ignored. With regard to sexual harassment, for example, research suggests that people who asked the person to stop or threatened to tell others reported more positive outcomes than those who ignored the behaviour. But, what if the conflict was confronted and the resolution attempt failed? In this case, it is important to review possible reasons for the failure as well as appraising future options.

WHY DO RESOLUTION ATTEMPTS FAIL?

Resolving a conflict is often easier said than done. We are rarely concerned with reconciliation or the methods of achieving it when we are angry with someone. Instead, we become preoccupied with winning. In addition to the difficulty of being able to deal rationally with a problem without letting emotions get in the way, there are three further reasons why resolution attempts fail. These are lack of motivation to resolve the conflict, the misinterpretation of resolution attempts and/or mismanagement of the attempt to resolve the conflict.

LACK OF MOTIVATION TO NEGOTIATE OR CHANGE

In order for an interpersonal conflict to be resolved, both parties have to have an incentive to do so. Without give-and-take, there can be no negotiation. There are two main reasons why one party to the dispute may lack motivation to negotiate or change. First, they might not regard themselves as having any responsibility for the conflict and hence believe that change is up to the other party. Second, they might feel that they stand to gain if the situation remains the same but would lose out if it changes. For example, what does the difficult boss, who misuses power in an attempt to control others, have to gain if behaviour change will result in a loss of this control? What does a colleague, who is trying to assert themselves over you, have to gain if they feel that behaviour involving power-plays is the best way to assert themselves? What does the dependent client, who seeks constant reassurance, have to gain if he or she no longer seeks your professional advice?

Clearly, one aim of conflict resolution is for both parties to recognize and accept that, in the long-term, no-one benefits from a conflictual relationship. The difficult boss will gain neither co-operation nor productivity from a dissatisfied subordinate. The emotional energy exerted in continuous battles between colleagues reduces the amount of energy which can be devoted to work. The demanding client will not learn to cope for themselves if they seek constant professional advice. Without mutual motivation for resolving the conflict, constructive dialogue will not be achieved.

MISPERCEPTION AND MISINTERPRETATION

As with any behaviour, resolution attempts are subject to misinterpretation or misperception by the other party. The difficult boss may perceive your action as questioning their authority; the awkward colleague may construe your action as game playing, that is, you are offering to negotiate but will not allow a satisfactory outcome to be reached; the dependent client may feel threatened or dismissed and could seek assistance from another professional. Even when one person is striving to be open about their feelings, opinions and intentions, these can be misread by others. In addition, some people unfortunately choose to misinterpret any action which they do not see as immediately favourable to themselves.

BADLY MANAGED ATTEMPTS TO RESOLVE THE CONFLICT

Resolution attempts might also fail because they were badly managed by yourself, the other party involved or by both of you. Perhaps you were too combative or competitive, too aggressive, threatening or impulsive; perhaps you failed to listen to the other person's point of view, seeking to blame them or put them down; perhaps you misread the situation; perhaps it was just poor timing. However, just as there are two sides to any conflict, so are there two sides to any failure to resolve the situation. As mentioned earlier, it is important to recognize the limits of your responsibility. If you believe you have worked hard to resolve the conflict, then should a conflict persist, it is the responsibility of both parties involved. Excessive self-blame can undermine your confidence, having an effect which is as damaging as the conflict itself.

If you feel you have done all you can to resolve a conflict with a boss, colleague or client and the conflict persists, you may well ask yourself, 'What next?'. There are a number of options you might pursue. You might wish to make one further attempt to resolve the conflict, make use of the conciliation services of a third party or review your options for working in an environment away from the person with whom you are in conflict.

OPTIONS WHEN CONFLICTS PERSIST

FURTHER ATTEMPTS TO RESOLVE THE CONFLICT

If you feel that you would like to make a further attempt to resolve the situation, it would be useful to delay this until any strong feelings have died down. This would give you time to review both the conflict and your approach to dealing with it, and enable you to gain a clearer impression of why the attempt failed and whether a further attempt would be desirable. A further attempt on your part may not be particularly rewarding if you feel the other party is unlikely to acknowledge that they have a part to play in the conflict or its resolution, or that they are determined to win at all costs. But a further attempt to resolve the conflict might well be justified if you feel your initial approach was more combative than collaborative or that you did not try as hard as you might have to solve the problem. You will also want to weigh up whether it would be better to make a further attempt or to try to live with the situation.

Advantages of making a further attempt:
- You would reassure yourself that you really have made the maximum effort to resolve the conflict.
- You would reduce the possibility of maintaining an awkward situation in which open conflict could develop at any time.
- It allows you to try alternative strategies.

Disadvantages of making a further attempt:
- The risk of 'losing' a second time with the possibility that this may undermine your confidence.
- The possibility that further failure may lead to a greater escalation of the conflict.

There are few clearly discernible advantages to trying to live with the situation. Although you may feel that making the best of a bad situation is your only remaining option, this is only likely to be viable if the conflict is relatively minor or if you do not work closely with the person concerned. In addition, trying to live with the situation still means that you will be left to cope with the negative effects of the initial conflict. Having confronted the situation and failed, there may now also be open hostility between you and the other party involved.

THIRD PARTY INTERVENTION

If your attempt to resolve the conflict did not involve the assistance of a third party, you may consider the use of a mediator a worthwhile course to pursue. The aim of a mediator should be to help both sides reach a settlement which advances both sets of interests. The third party should not force the two parties to resolve their disagreement; a coercive solution is unlikely to address concerns or lead to an enduring or satisfactory outcome. A manager who determines what issues need to be settled and then decides their outcome may well establish a pattern of future dependence, with subordinates bringing every conflict to their boss for a decision about who is right. The aim of mediation should be to encourage compromise and bargaining and to work towards a collaborative and workable Win–Win solution rather than a combative Win–Lose outcome.

A third party can thus set the agenda; facilitate constructive communication between the parties; focus on objective issues in the conflict; and enable parties to retreat gracefully and to 'save-face'.

The last point can be particularly important for it is the task of the mediator to substitute the notion of 'losing a conflict' with that of 'negotiating a settlement'. No-one likes to lose face in the eyes of superiors, colleagues, clients or any other person with whom one is in conflict. The third party can control the pace of 'retreat' and take responsibility for any concessions made. If the two parties arrive at an impasse, a good mediator would encourage them to make concessions so that neither party would be able to attribute blame to the other for coercion or pressure.

In any organization, there are a variety of people who could act as third parties, perhaps using existing dispute resolution procedures. These include union or professional representatives; those trusted to reconcile differences, such as valued colleagues; those with more power such as immediate superiors or managers who, when all else has failed, can impose a settlement. Although unsatisfactory, such an outside directive can sometimes paper over the cracks.

Who is approached will depend upon the nature of the conflict. If the conflict is with a boss or a client, then it might be appropriate to approach one's union or a professional body. If the conflict is with a colleague then, in the first instance, it is appropriate to approach one's immediate superior. If the third party is someone from within the organization, they are more likely to be effective if they are detached from the dispute and its resolution.

A third party:
- should have little prior knowledge of the background issues involved – a mediator divorced from the conflict's history is more likely to gain a clear and impartial view of the situation;
- should have no vested interest in the outcome – a mediator should be free to guide both parties to a mutually acceptable outcome;
- should be able to control the setting and the process involved – a mediator should be free to select venues and be unencumbered by time contraints for the settlement of the conflict;
- should have little power over the actual fate of the parties concerned – a mediator should not impose a settlement or be able to use the conflict to the participants' subsequent detriment.

If the third party is a colleague, it may be more difficult for them to have sufficient control over the setting or the process, or to remain disinterested in the outcome. They are also more likely to be perceived as having knowledge of the history of the conflict and the issues involved. Although superiors may have more expertise and control over the setting and process, they may well have some power over the fate of those involved and hence might be perceived as not being entirely neutral.

Clearly, any third party must be perceived by both parties involved as credible and neutral. In deciding whom to approach, one question to ask is, 'Do they have the appropriate authority over and respect of each person involved in the conflict?'. There would be little point for someone to turn to their boss for help in resolving a conflict with a colleague, even though this might be the appropriate first step, if both parties know that their boss has limited past success in resolving such disputes. Unfortunately, as shown in Chapter 3, managers frequently encourage denial and avoidance. A further question is, 'Does the third party have any particular commitment to either party?'. Clearly the only interest a mediator should have is in a mutually satisfactory resolution to a conflict and not in supporting one or other of the parties involved.

If there is any indication that the mediator is biased towards a particular outcome, this would severely limit an effective resolution to the problem. It is usually best for the third party to have a similar professional and personal relationship with each party to the conflict, for example, being an immediate superior or a person who spends a comparable amount of time with and has a similar regard for each party to the conflict.

MEDIATING SKILLS

Not everyone who is in a position to intervene in a conflict will possess equally effective conflict management skills. Wehr (1979) has identified the following ten skills as being essential to peacemaking.

- *Conflict analysis.* As noted in previous chapters, parties in conflict frequently lose sight of the issues. A good mediator has the ability to clarify the issues involved, helping the parties to establish the real facts about the problem.

- *Empathy.* Given that both parties will almost inevitably perceive the same events in a very different way, the good mediator has the ability to understand each party's position.

- *Listening.* The mediator can act as a referee, making sure that both parties state their views and have the opportunity to vent their anger, resentment and frustration. In interpersonal conflicts, the expressing of emotions can reduce hostility so that the issues can be addressed.

- *Sense of timing.* It is unlikely that an enduring interpersonal conflict will be resolved rapidly. Both parties will require time to talk, to express how they feel and to think about the situation. It may be necessary to proceed in stages and the mediator thus requires the ability to judge when and how to proceed with negotiations.

- *Trust and credibility.* As noted above, it is important for the mediator to be seen as objective, credible and trustworthy by both parties.

- *Mediation.* There are a range of skills that the mediator can use to help facilitate the process of negotiation. These include helping both parties to recognize that they can achieve a 'Win–Win', collaborative solution and that it is not necessary for someone to lose for the other party to win; helping both parties to see when they are blaming or putting each other down; helping both parties to acknowledge common ground and to search for alternative solutions.

- *Communication.* Interpersonal conflict is characterized by hostile communication. If third party mediators can reduce the level of threat and increase the amount of trust, the chances of resolving the conflict are also increased. Facilitating communication is always a first step towards resolving interpersonal conflict.

- *Imagination.* Even with the assistance of a mediator, the process of conflict resolution will not be smooth. There always will be an occasional impasse which can only be eliminated by the ability to think of creative alternative solutions.

- *Joint-costing.* The mediator can encourage the parties to assess the costs of continuing in conflict and the potential benefits of resolving it.

- *Crisis management.* At their extreme, interpersonal conflicts at work may engender overt hostility and aggression between the two parties concerned. Initial crisis management might involve immediate intervention, such as imposing temporary rules for communication or allowing the parties to work separately for a short time.

Unfortunately, not all mediators possess these skills and a suitable third party may not be available. If the conflict is left to fester, it could become a constant source of resentment, accusations, complaints and lowered morale. A point may come when the only remaining option is to consider leaving your job.

REVIEWING WORK-RELATED OPTIONS

Should all else fail, you may wish to review your options for working in an environment away from the person with whom you have the conflict. It might be possible to seek a transfer to a different department, ward or office or you may have to consider leaving your current employment. Transferring your job within the company will depend both upon the availability of a suitable alternative, as well as the willingness of those in positions of authority to facilitate such a move.

A decision to leave your job is clearly not to be taken lightly,

CHECKLIST: WHEN CONFLICTS PERSIST

EXERCISE 9

This exercise is designed to provide you with the opportunity to explore and think about the available options you might pursue if a conflict persists. Work through each of the sections, thinking carefully about your answers. Discuss them with a friend, colleague or partner if possible.

1. Did you ignore or confront the initial conflict?

(i) If you ignored it, ask yourself:

- *Did I consider the initial conflict to be trivial?*
- *Have I dwelt on the situation?*
- *Have I felt angry or tense as a result of the conflict?*
- *Has the conflict become more distressing?*

[If your answer is 'yes' to at least two of these questions, it might now be necessary to confront the conflict head on.]

(ii) If you confronted the initial conflict but your resolution attempts failed, ask yourself:

- *Was there a lack of motivation to change on the part of the other party?*
- *Did they misperceive or misinterpret my resolution attempts?*
- *Was I too combative or competitive?*
- *Did I fail to listen to the other person's point of view?*
- *Did I misread the situation?*
- *Was it just poor timing?*

[The reasons for the failure are likely to influence your subsequent action; perceived failure on your part (a 'yes' answer to the last four questions) is easier to modify than a perceived failure on the part of the other party involved (a 'yes' answer to the first two questions). The former may prompt you to make a further attempt to resolve the situation, the latter may prompt you to involve a third party or to review your work-related options.]

2. What should you do next?

(i) Should you make a further attempt to resolve the conflict?

Ask yourself:

- *Is the other party likely to change?*
- *Are they likely to acknowledge that they have a part to play in the conflict and its resolution?*
- *Are they determined to win at all costs?*
- *Was my approach truly collaborative or was it combative?*
- *Have I tried my hardest to solve the problem?*

[A 'no' answer to either of the first two questions or a 'yes' answer to the the third question suggests that a further attempt may also be unsuccessful; a 'no' answer to the latter two questions may prompt you to examine your own approach to the problem and to try once more.]

(ii) Should you seek third party involvement?

Ask yourself:

- *Should I turn to someone to advise or represent me?*
- *What do people in my organization do if they have a complaint?*
- *With whom, if anyone, should I raise the issue?*
- *What happens if I approach someone over this issue?*
- *Will I be able to air my grievances fully?*
- *Will I be able to shape the outcome?*
- *Is there a strong likelihood of a satisfactory settlement?*
- *Are there specific procedures available for such issues?*

[If the situation has reached an impasse and your answers to the last four questions are positive, then mediation might be the answer. If the conflict is with a colleague, then it is usual to approach one's immediate boss in the first instance. If this is not a viable option, or if the conflict is with your boss, then an approach can be made to your trade union or professional body.]

3. Should you review work-related options?

When all attempts to resolve a conflict have failed and you have pursued every available option fully, there may be few alternatives open to you. Ask yourself:

- *Have I tried every possible option?*
- *Is the situation affecting my health?*
- *Is the situation making me more irritable and/or depressed?*

[If the answer to each of these questions is 'yes', then you may wish to review your options. Make a list of the advantages and disadvantages of remaining in your current employment. You may find it helpful to discuss your list with a close friend or your partner. It may well be that one advantage, perhaps financial reward, outweighs a fairly substantive list of disadvantages.]

Ask yourself:

- *If there are clear rewards to the job, could these be obtained elsewhere?*
- *What other forms of employment are available?*
- *What would the chances be of obtaining alternative employment?*

If you have pursued all other options and there are real opportunities elsewhere, then changing jobs may well be the best course to pursue.

although this is certainly an option pursued by many people. As noted in the previous chapter, as many as one-fifth of those who are the victims of sexual harassment, take this action. The viability of this option will depend on a range of factors. Many people may find it difficult to leave a situation with which they are familiar, feeling that it is better the devil they know than the devil they don't know. Others may feel that leaving a job as a result of interpersonal conflict is a sign of defeat. Perhaps the foremost factor in determining whether to change jobs or not is the amount of personal distress caused by the conflict. Anyone experiencing extreme irritability, nervousness, depression and stress-related physical illnesses as a result of interpersonal conflicts at work, may well consider their health to be more important than their job. For many people, however, the most important factor for staying is financial considerations. Many tolerate unsatisfactory and stressful situations at work because of the need for an income to maintain family and home. Unfortunately, however, such considerations frequently prevent people from making any realistic appraisals of alternatives. It is important to try to step back from the situation and assess as objectively as possible whether other forms of employment might be available, and what the chances would be of obtaining alternative employment.

Even if attempts to resolve a conflict fail, conflicts can still have positive outcomes. They can lead to a clearer understanding both of ourselves and of other people. If you have made every effort to confront the conflict, you can feel confident about your self-worth even if your resolution attempts have failed. If, as a result, you carefully and systematically evaluate your work-related options, this can also be for the good. We frequently become complacent about our situation, and require a jolt to force us to appraise our options. As long as the re-evaluation is systematic and thorough, it can lead to a new, more satisfactory life plan. It is only when we look back that we think, 'Why did I not make this move before?'.

REFERENCES

Argyle, M. and Henderson, M. (1985) *The Anatomy of Relationships*. Harmondsworth: Penguin.

Bannister, V.G. (1991) Sexual harassment: legal issues, past and future developments. In M.J. Davidson and J. Earnshaw (Eds) *Vulnerable Workers: Psychosocial and Legal Issues*. Chichester: John Wiley.

Berne, E. (1964) *Games People Play: The Psychology of Human Relationships*. Harmondsworth: Penguin.

Breakwell, G.M. (1989) *Facing Physical Violence*. London: BPS Books (British Psychological Society) and Routledge.

Brown, C. and Gay, P. (1985) *Racial Discrimination 17 Years after the Act*. London: Policy Studies Institute.

Crull, P. (1982) Stress effects of sexual harassment on the job: Implications for counselling. *American Journal of Orthopsychiatry, 52*, 539–544.

D'Augelli, A.R. (1989) Lesbians' and gay men's experiences of discrimination and harassment in a university community. *American Journal of Community Psychology, 17*, 317–321.

Davidson, M.J. and Earnshaw, J. (1990) Policies, practices and attitudes towards sexual harassment in U.K. organisations. *Personnel Review, 19*, 23–27.

Deutsch, M. (1971) Toward an understanding of conflict. *International Journal of Group Tensions, 1*, 42–54.

Fontana, D. (1989) *Managing Stress*. London: BPS Books (British Psychological Society) and Routledge.

Fontana, D. (1990) *Social Skills at Work*. London: BPS Books (British Psychological Society) and Routledge.

Glaser, R.D. and Thorpe, J.S. (1986) Unethical intimacy: A survey of sexual contact and advances between psychology educators and female graduate students. *American Psychologist, 41*, 43–51.

Groves, J. (1978) Taking care of the hateful patient. *New England Journal of Medicine, 298*, 883–887.

Gutek, B.A. (1985) *Sex and the Workplace: The Impact of Sexual Behavior and Harassment on Women, Men and Organisations*. San Francisco: Jossey-Bass.

Gutek, B.A. and Morasch, B. (1982) Sex ratios, sex role spillover and sexual harassment of women at work. *Journal of Social Issues, 38*, 55–74.

Holroyd, J.C. and Brodsky, A.M. (1977) Psychologists' attitudes and practices regarding erotic and nonerotic physical contact with patients. *American Psychologist, 32*, 843–849.

Kanter, R. (1979) *Men and Women of the Corporation*. New York: Basic Books.

Loy, P.H. and Stewart, L.P. (1984) The extent and effects of the sexual harassment of working women. *Sociological Forces, 17*, 31–43.

Mintzberg, H. (1973) *The Nature of Managerial Work*. New York: Harper & Row.

Pope, K.S. (1988) How clients are harmed by sexual contact with mental health professionals: The syndrome and its prevalence. *Journal of Counselling and Development, 67*, 222–226.

Rhodes, S. (1983) Age-related differences in work attitudes and behaviour: A review. *Psychological Bulletin, 97*, 328–326.

Rowe, M.T. (1981) Dealing with sexual harassment. *Harvard Business Review*, 59, 42–46.

Rusbult, C.E. (1983) A longitudinal test of the investment model: The development (and deterioration) of satisfaction and commitment in heterosexual investments. *Journal of Personality and Social Psychology*, 45, 101–117.

Sayles, M. (1964) *Managerial Behavior*. New York: McGraw-Hill.

Steiner, C.M. (1981) *The Other Side of Power*. New York: Grove Press.

Stewart, R. (1967) *Managers and their Jobs*. London: MacMillan.

Stockdale, J.E. (1991) Sexual harassment at work. In J. Firth-Cozens and M.A. West (Eds) *Women at Work*. Milton Keynes: Oxford University Press.

Terpstra, D.E. and Baker, D.D. (1991) Sexual harassment at work: The psychosocial issues. In M. J. Davidson and J. Earnshaw (Eds) *Vulnerable Workers: Psychosocial and Legal Issues*. Chichester: John Wiley.

Terpstra, D.E. and Cook, S.E. (1985) Complainant characteristics and reported behaviors and consequences associated with formal sexual harassment charges. *Personnel Psychology*, 38, 559–574.

US Merit Systems Protection Board (1981) *Sexual Harassment in the Federal Workplace: Is it a Problem?* Washington DC: US Government Printing Office.

US Merit Systems Protection Board (1988) *Sexual Harassment in the Federal Government: An Update*. Washington DC: US Government Printing Office.

Walster, E.H., Walster, G.W. and Berscheid, E. (1978) *Equity Theory and Research*. Boston: Allyn & Bacon.

Wehr, P. (1979) *Conflict Regulation*. Boulder, Colorado: Westview Press.

FURTHER READING

Argyle, M. (1981) *Social Skills and Work*. London: Methuen.
A useful, if slightly dated, textbook for professionals, summarizing research pertaining to skills required for a range of tasks in a variety of work contexts.

Back, K., Back, K. and Bates, T. (1991) *Assertiveness at Work: A Practical Guide to Handling Awkward Situations*, 2nd ed. London: McGraw-Hill.
A straightforward, readable and practical guide on how to be assertive at work.

Cooper, C.L. and Payne, R. (1978) *Stress at Work*. Chichester: John Wiley & Sons.
A slightly dated but readable textbook reviewing the main factors relating to stress at work.

Davidson, M.J. and Earnshaw, J. (Eds) (1991) *Vulnerable workers: Psychological and Legal Issues*. Chichester: John Wiley & Sons.
The chapters in this textbook present up-to-date reviews of the

literature relating to the difficulties experienced by 'vulnerable' groups at work. Particularly pertinent chapters deal with psychosocial and legal issues pertaining to sexual harassment, the experience of black workers and lesbians and gay men in the workplace.

Fisher, R. and Ury, W. (1986) *Getting to Yes. Negotiating Agreement Without Giving In*. London: Hutchinson Business Books Ltd.
A generally readable guide detailing a practical method for negotiating agreement amicably, written by two of the leading authorities in the field. No subject index.

Gutek, B.A. (1985) *Sex and the Workplace: The Impact of Sexual Behavior and Harassment on Women, Men and Organisations*. San Francisco: Jossey-Bass.
An important and frequently cited text in the area. This readable book reviews both the relevant theory and research, including the author's own.

Hinde, R.A. (1979) *Towards Understanding Relationships*. London: Academic Press.
Even though this is a slightly dated academic text, it is nevertheless a readable review of research and issues relating to relationships in general.

Leavitt, H.J. and Bahrami, H. (1988) *Managerial Psychology. Managing Behavior in Organizations*, 5th ed. Chicago: University of Chicago Press.
A widely used textbook in organizational psychology.

Marshall, J. (1986) *Women Managers: Travellers in a Male World*. Chichester: John Wiley & Sons.
A readable textbook reviewing the research pertaining to the main issues and problems encountered by women managers.

Nelson-Jones, R. (1986) *Human Relationship Skills. Training and Self Help*. Sydney: Holt, Rinehart and Winston.
Written by a counselling psychologist, this clear practical guide has over 70 exercises designed to help the reader to develop their relationship skills.

Walton, R.E. (1987) *Managing Conflict. Interpersonal Dialogue and Third-party Roles*. Reading, Massachusetts: Addison-Wesley.
Based upon three case histories of interpersonal conflict, this book presents an analysis of third party functions, tactics and role attributes. No subject index.

INDEX